"Christopher Wright has given us a powe[...] idolatry both in biblical times and today. [...] dangers of political idolatry, which has [...] Importantly, he not only diagnoses the pr[...] [...]edy. This book should be a must-read for Christians as they engage with the political process."

Tremper Longman III, author of *The Bible and the Ballot: Using Scripture in Political Decision*

"Wright's careful dive into Scripture on the meaning of idolatry packs a punch for our times—an important reminder that idols, including political idols, are false gods that we create in our image, capable of great harm and destruction but ultimately ciphers within the true created order."

John Inazu, Sally D. Danforth Distinguished Professor of Law and Religion at Washington University in St. Louis

"The biblical warning to 'keep yourselves from idols' homes in on the source of spiritual, social, moral, and existential ruin. Chris Wright's fine study on idolatry in Scripture and his application of it to our Western world shines a bright light to help us see more clearly what is at stake. Although the West has been shaped by many (now-fading) biblical ideals, we are witnessing a culture shot through with a host of idolatrous tendencies to put our trust in the wrong places—in that which is not-God. Whatever our political views as Christians may be, Wright offers correctives for all of us, exhorting us to be guided by biblical priorities and Christ-centered discipleship, which will ultimately lead to our flourishing as God's image-bearers."

Paul Copan, Pledger Family Chair of Philosophy and Ethics at Palm Beach Atlantic University, coauthor of *Introduction to Biblical Ethics*

"Chris Wright offers a biblically and theologically grounded, unsparing analysis of the idolatrous character of contemporary Western Christianity, formed in collusion with our wider cultures. His focus on idolatry bears on Christian thought and practice in areas as seemingly diverse as mission, creation care, justice work, addiction treatment, and the cultivation of theological maturity and ethical integrity. This timely book is a sobering call to repentance and the renewal of Christian vocation."

Ellen F. Davis, Amos Ragan Kearns Distinguished Professor of Bible and Practical Theology at Duke Divinity School

"Fearless, provocative, clear, direct, sharp, urgent, wide-horizoned: it was all those things when he wrote it. But in light of subsequent events, by the time it's published it is a tract for the times."

John Goldingay, senior professor of Old Testament at Fuller Theological Seminary, author of *Old Testament Ethics*

"Communal idolatry is one of the most fundamental ways the Bible speaks of human rebellion and sin. Our failure to recognize this has had a crippling effect on the mission of the church in a world rife with idolatry. We have here a very helpful treatment of this theme, grounded in a careful reading of the biblical text and aimed at equipping God's people for its mission in today's world. I am deeply thankful to God for Chris Wright and his faithful and relevant scholarship, which is such a gift to the church today."

Michael W. Goheen, professor of missional theology at Covenant Seminary, St Louis, and director of theological education at Missional Training Center, Phoenix

"A scathing indictment of the gods of the West—idols we (you and I) have built with our own hands and inadvertently worship. The power and persuasiveness of Wright's prophetic work lies not in bombastic words (he's as irenic as ever) but in the convincing and gripping connection the author makes between idolatry back then and idolatry that we participate in within our present world. The strangeness of this journey between two worlds often leaves Westerners unconvinced about anything but glib connections. Christopher Wright's *"Here Are Your Gods"* shatters our shallow readings of Scripture. It will leave you with deeply rooted convictions and, alas, a thoroughly uneasy feeling about false temples and idols that we have built. A most timely evangelical critique of Western society and politics!"

William J. Webb, adjunct professor of biblical studies at Tyndale Seminary in Toronto, coauthor of *Bloody, Brutal, and Barbaric?*

CHRISTOPHER J. H. WRIGHT

'HERE ARE YOUR GODS!'

FAITHFUL DISCIPLESHIP IN IDOLATROUS TIMES

INTER-VARSITY PRESS
36 Causton Street, London SW1P 4ST, England
Email: ivp@ivpbooks.com
Website: www.ivpbooks.com

© Christopher J. H. Wright, 2020

Content in part one is adapted from chapter five of Christopher J. H. Wright, *The Mission of God:
Unlocking the Bible's grand narrative* (Downers Grove, IL: InterVarsity Press, 2006).
Used with permission.

*First published in the United States of America in 2020
by InterVarsity Press, Downers Grove, Illinois*

*First published in Great Britain in 2020
by Inter-Varsity Press*

British Library Cataloguing-in-Publication Data
A catalogue record for this book is available from the British Library.

ISBN: 978–1–78974–231–2
eBook ISBN: 978–1–78974–232–9

Set in Arno Pro 11/15 pt
Typeset in Great Britain by CRB Associates, Potterhanworth, Lincolnshire
Printed in Great Britain by Ashford Colour Press Ltd, Gosport, Hampshire

Contents

Preface

THIS BOOK IS A COMBINATION of two sources. Part one is a slightly edited and adapted version of "The Living God Confronts Idolatry," from my *The Mission of God: Unlocking the Bible's Grand Narrative*. The topic of idolatry is so important that this material is present in a new form and publication. It serves as the foundation for part two.

The origin of the remaining chapters in part two lies in an invitation I received to deliver a public lecture in St. Michael's Church, Charleston, South Carolina, on January 11, 2017. This was during a week I spent sharing the Bible teaching at the Anglican Leadership Institute in Charleston with a group of church leaders from other countries at the invitation of Rev. Dr. Peter Moore. The title for my lecture, proposed by Dr. Moore, was "Following Jesus in an Age of Political Turbulence." That it was a lecture also accounts for the slight shift to a more applied style in part two, reflecting the nature of the occasion on which it was delivered.

The reason for the invitation and the lecture title was that many of us were (and still are) staggering with a mixture of baffled incomprehension and alarm at the two major events in the United Kingdom and the United States in 2016: the referendum over the United Kingdom's membership in the European Union, which ended in a narrow victory for Brexit, in June; and the election of Donald Trump to the office of president of the United States in November. What is going on in the world that such things happen—things that many people not so long ago would have thought to be almost unimaginable? Of course, things have moved on a lot since those two events of 2016, and we shall consider wider examples of national idolatry. But they were the trigger for the reflections in part two. This book was written, of course, before the onset and devastating spread of the Covid-19 pandemic, though the final stages of its editing have happened while that scourge is still afflicting the world. To the extent that this global crisis is at least in part the outcome of human folly and the human arrogance and idolatry that accompany and exacerbate such folly, the theme of the book seems even more sharply pertinent.

I am grateful to Glenn Shrom for repeatedly urging me to consider publishing the chapter on idolatry in *The Mission of God* as a separate book; also to InterVarsity Press (USA) and Inter-Varsity Press (UK) for permission to republish it in this form; to Anna Gissing for most helpful collaboration in the editorial challenge of blending the various materials together; and to Pieter Kwant, my agent, for encouraging the publication of the lecture and other materials in part two. I am well aware that there are other much more profound and insightful analyses of contemporary idolatries in our Western culture. Some of these are listed in the footnotes in part one. The most recent such analysis, with a solidly biblical foundation and missional challenge, sets the radical claims of biblical monotheism in stark contrast to the idolatries of our culture. It is provided by Bruce Ashford and Heath Thomas in *The Gospel of Our King: Bible, Worldview, and the Mission of Every Christian* (Grand Rapids: Baker Academic, 2019).

Part one

THE LORD GOD AND OTHER GODS IN THE BIBLE

MONOTHEISM AND MISSION. Two vast words that you will not actually find in the Bible, yet they embrace massive biblical teaching: that there is only one true living God, the God revealed as Yahweh in the Old Testament and incarnated in Jesus of Nazareth in the New; and that this God revealed in the Bible is on mission, that is to say, he is working out his own sovereign plan and purpose for the whole creation through the whole of human history and calls his whole redeemed people to participate with him in that mission.

Each of these words, *monotheism* and *mission*, is inseparably tied to the other.

Biblical monotheism is necessarily missional. That is because the one true living God of the biblical revelation wills to be known and worshiped throughout his whole creation and by all the nations of humanity. That divine will to be known constitutes and generates the mission of God, through biblical history and to the end of human history.

And biblical mission is necessarily monotheistic. That is because God's people are commissioned to call people of all nations to the worship of this one living Creator and Redeemer God, and to join all creation in giving this one God the praise and glory that is due to him alone.[1]

What about all the other gods that populate the pages of the Bible and surround us still today in many forms? In the four chapters of part one we will examine how the Bible handles the phenomenon of human beings worshiping many alleged deities other than the God of Israel. What exactly are they? What should be a missional response to this phenomenon? What should we be doing in relation to idols and gods?

It has long seemed to me that the biblical category of *idolatry*—when it is even considered at all—is often handled or dismissed with shallow understanding and simplistic responses. Yet surely it is a fundamental, though negative, aspect of a fully biblical and missional account of biblical monotheism. For that reason, we should make an effort to grapple with how the Bible handles the subject, as a vital part of authentic and sensitive Christian mission.

CHAPTER ONE

THE PARADOX
OF THE GODS

A RE THE "OTHER GODS" that we read about in the Bible something or nothing?

A statue is real enough. A carved or molten image has three-dimensional existence in the real world. But what about the god or gods those images supposedly represent? Are they real? Do they exist? Are they something or nothing? What did Israel believe about the gods in relation to its own God, Yahweh?

That last question has vexed the minds of Old Testament theologians for many decades. With monotheism defined, in the generic categories of human religion, as the belief that only one divine entity exists, along with the consequent denial of the existence of any other deities whatsoever, the search was on for the process by which and the time by when Israel could be said to have achieved monotheism in that sense. Clearly Israelites expressed their commitment to Yahweh in some very exclusive terms. But did that mean that Israelites categorically denied the *existence* of the other gods whom they were forbidden to worship?

The classic answer given within the guild of Old Testament scholarship has been the evolutionary or developmental one summarized, repackaged, and reissued by Robert Gnuse.[1] With variations as to the precise dating of the transitions, this view reconstructs the religious history of Israel as proceeding from (1) polytheism (as conceded in Josh 24:14), through (2) henotheism (or mono-Yahwism, the demand for exclusive worship of Yahweh *by Israel*, while accepting the existence of the gods of other nations), to (3) true monotheism (the explicit denial of the existence of any other gods than Yahweh) as a final and fairly late conclusion of the process.

According to some scholars, the first and second stages span most of the Old Testament history of Israel. That is, they argue, originally Israelite religion was virtually indistinguishable from Canaanite religion. Then for centuries the major drive within Israel was merely to get Israel to be loyal to its national covenant with Yahweh and not "go after other gods." The other gods that they might be tempted to go after were clearly presumed to exist. Yair Hoffman, for example, argues that even in the Deuteronomic traditions, the characteristic phrase 'ĕlōhîm ăḥērîm, "other gods," presumes, rather than denies, their existence as gods. "The phrase . . . although reflecting some idea of otherness, does not certify that these deities were considered an utterly different essence from the God of Israel. . . . They are *other* gods since they are not *ours*."[2] Finally, only in the late exile (to which Is 40–55 is assigned), did anyone in Israel say in so many words that no other god than Yahweh even existed.[3] Only at that final stage was it envisaged that the category of deity was a house with one sole and exclusive occupant—Yahweh.

On this view, the answer to our question about whether, in the religion of Israel, other gods actually existed depends on the point in the chronological development of Israel at which the question is asked. Suppose you could have approached an Israelite and asked, "Do you believe that there are other gods as well as Yahweh?" For a long period, the answer you would have received (according to the critical consensus) would have been, "Of course. There are many gods. Yahweh is one of the gods and a very powerful one, so we're rather glad he's our god." Then, when the more exclusive ideas of a national covenant were introduced and emphasized by the prophets and the reforming Deuteronomistic party, the answer would have been, "Yes, other nations have their own gods, but Yahweh is the only God that *Israel* must worship, or we will face the consequences of his anger." That view clashed with a more liberal, popular polytheism for a long time. Finally, however, with the triumph of the "official" Yahwistic party in the late exilic and postexilic period, the answer eventually would have been a firm, "No, Yahweh alone is 'the God,' and other gods have no real existence at all. All so-called gods are actually nonentities."

Such a neat linear view, however, is almost certainly just that—too neat. It is far too simple to put the question (or its answer) in a simple binary form: Do other gods exist, or do they not exist? Are they something or nothing? The issue is more complex and depends on the predicate of such questions (that is to say, to what does the word *god* refer to?). What needs to be added to the question is "Do other gods exist within *the same order of existence that Yahweh does*?" "Are they the same 'thing' as Yahweh is [the same divine 'something']? Or are they not what Yahweh is ['no-thing,' i.e., no-divine-thing]?"

Now, we can tell from reading multiple Old Testament texts that the essence of Israelite monotheism lies in what Israel affirmed dynamically about Yahweh (namely, that Yahweh alone is the universal *Creator*, the sovereign *Ruler* of all histories, the *Judge* of all nations, and the *Savior* of people from all nations who turn to him), not primarily in what it denied about other gods. Nevertheless, what the Old Testament affirms about Yahweh has unavoidable negative consequences for whatever may be claimed about other gods. Commenting particularly on Deuteronomy, and disputing Nathan MacDonald's argument that the book does not deny the existence of other gods (and is therefore not formally monotheistic, in terms of the Enlightenment categories that MacDonald rightly rejects as irrelevant and damaging in Old Testament study), Richard Bauckham makes the following carefully nuanced point (the references are to Deuteronomy):

> What Israel is able to recognize about Yahweh, from his acts for Israel, that distinguishes Yahweh from the gods of the nations is that he is "the God" or "the god of gods." This means primarily that he has unrivalled power throughout the cosmos. The earth, the heavens and the heaven of heavens belong to him (10:14). By

contrast, the gods of the nations are impotent nonentities, who cannot protect and deliver even their own peoples. This is the message of the song of Moses (see especially 32:37-39). The need to distinguish among "the gods" between the one who is supreme (Yahweh) and the others who are not just subordinate but powerless, creates, on the one hand, the usages "the God" and "the god of gods," and, on the other hand, the contemptuous "non-god" (32:17: לֹא אֱלֹהַ; 32:21: לֹא אֵל), and "their mere puffs of air" (32:21: הַבְלֵיהֶם). Though called gods, the other gods do not really deserve the term, because they are not *effective* divinities acting with power in the world. Yahweh alone is the God with supreme power . . . (32:39). . . . It is not enough to observe that Deuteronomy does not deny the *existence* of other gods. We should also recognize that, once we do attend to the ontological implications that MacDonald admits Deuteronomy's "doctrine of God" must have, this theology is driving an ontological division through the midst of the old category "gods" such that Yahweh appears in a class of his own.[4]

So, coming back to the question, are the gods something or nothing? If the question is asked *in relation to Yahweh*, the answer has to be *nothing*. Nothing whatsoever compares with Yahweh or stands in the same category as he does. Yahweh is not one of a generic category—"the gods." Yahweh alone is *the* God, in what Bauckham calls "transcendent uniqueness."[5] With reference to Yair Hoffman's point above: while it may be true to say that the phrase "other gods" does not by itself imply that "these deities were considered an utterly different essence from the God of Israel," nevertheless what is said about Yahweh makes it categorically clear that *he* is of an utterly different essence from *them*. "Yahweh, he is the God; there is no other beside him" (Deut 4:35, my translation).

But if the question is asked *in relation to those who worship* the other gods—whether the nations who claimed them as their own national deities, or even if asked in relation to the temptation that Israel faced to go after them—then the answer can certainly be *something*. The gods of the nations, with their names, statues, myths, and cults, clearly did have an existence in the life, culture, and history of those who treated them as their gods. It is not nonsense to form sentences such as "Marduk was a god worshiped by the people of Babylon." Only excessive pedantry would complain that since Marduk did not have any real divine existence it is meaningless to say that anybody worshiped him. In the context of such a sentence (and all similar descriptions of human religions), it makes understandable sense to talk about other gods as something—something that exists in the world of human experience. In other words, it is not impossible, theologically or in ordinary discourse, to answer the question "Are other gods something or nothing?" with the paradox "Both." They are *nothing in relation to Yahweh*; they are *something in relation to their worshipers*.

This is precisely the paradox that Paul carefully articulates in his response to the problem of meat sacrificed to idols in Corinth. Paul agrees with the creedal affirmation of those who based their freedom in the matter on the Jewish Shema. There is only one God and Lord, and so "an idol is nothing at all in the world" (1 Cor 8:4). Yet in the next sentence Paul can go on, "For even if there are so-called gods, whether in heaven or on earth (as indeed there are many 'gods' and many 'lords')" (1 Cor 8:5). In other words, Paul accepts there is *something* there, even if it is not in any sense equivalent to the one God, the Father, and the one Lord, Jesus Christ. What that something actually is, Paul (and we) will return to. But his double assertion is clear enough: gods and idols do exist; but they do not have the *divine* existence that the one living God alone possesses.

If Paul, a first-century Jew, basing his whole theological worldview on the Scriptures we call the Old Testament, could sustain this dual perspective, there seems no reason why it would have been impossible for those who shared his faith in preceding centuries to have held a similar paradox quite comfortably. It is clearly the perspective of the great polemical chapters of Isaiah 40–48, for example. From Yahweh's point of view, expressed in the soaring poetry of the prophet, the gods are simply "less than nothing . . . utterly worthless" (Is 41:24). Yet from the point of view of the exiles with their cowering inferiority complex, the gods of Babylon can be challenged to come into court and be exposed there as powerless (Is 41:21-24), can be mocked as human artifacts (Is 44:9-20), and can be caricatured as stooping down from heaven in a futile attempt to save not their worshipers, to whom they are now a useless burden, but their own idols (Is 46:1-2). All of this rhetoric is expended on the gods because they are something—something that Israel must see for what it is and be freed from; something that must be debunked and dismissed, so that it no longer stands in the way of Israel's restoration to the worship of its living Redeemer God.

What was possible for the prophet was surely no less possible for the author of a book of such theological depth and subtlety as Deuteronomy. Indeed, we find the same paradoxical duality. On the one hand, other gods are nothing when the point of reference or comparison is Yahweh. I can find no other way to understand the following affirmations than that they simply mean what they say: Yahweh alone is transcendently God, the sole owner and ruler of the universe.

> The LORD is God in heaven above and on the earth below. There is no other. (Deut 4:39)

> To the LORD your God belong the heavens, even the highest heavens, the earth and everything in it. (Deut 10:14)

> The LORD your God is God of gods and Lord of lords, the great God. (Deut 10:17)

> See now that I myself am he!
>   There is no god besides me.
> I put to death and I bring to life,
>   I have wounded and I will heal,
>   and no one can deliver out of my hand. (Deut 32:39)

In the context of such affirmations, the question as to what other gods may be receives its verdict: they are "not God" (Deut 32:17), "what is no God" (Deut 32:21). In short, *nothing*—nothing in comparison to Yahweh.

Yet, on the other hand, the same book, contemplating the enticing attractiveness and seductive power of the religious culture that lay ahead of Israel when it crossed the Jordan (the gods and idols, sacred places, the male and female fertility symbols, the apparent success of a whole civilization based on serving these gods), knew that in warning Israel repeatedly to avoid such idolatry, was warning it against *something*—something that was very real and very dangerous. Furthermore, to the extent that other nations worshiped heavenly bodies, the objects of their worship were certainly something with real existence—"the sun, the moon and the stars—all the heavenly array" (Deut 4:19). Israel was not to worship them because they are part of the created order, and as such Yahweh had assigned them "to all the nations under heaven"—not intending them to be worshiped but to be enjoyed for their created purpose as light givers.[6]

So then, it seems a futile exercise to attempt to unravel the Old Testament documents and lay them out along a line of progressive religious development, on the flawed assumption that people who speak about other gods as if they existed in some sense could not at the same time have believed that Yahweh alone is God. The logical conclusion of such an argument would be that once you become convinced of monotheism you should never again even speak about other gods, lest you be thought to be granting them real existence as divine. Yet that would be an absurd restriction on theological discourse. How then could Paul have even discussed the relationship between the living God and the gods and idols of the world in which his mission took place? Are we to say that because Paul refers to these things, in order to critique them, he must have believed in their existence in some sense comparable to the divine reality of the living God of Israel revealed in Christ? We have Paul's own word for it that he assuredly did not mean that. Yet Old Testament scholars repeatedly allege that simply by *referring* to the gods of the nations around them the Israelites must have *believed* in their real existence on a par with Yahweh.

What was true for Paul is equally true for us as contemporary Christians. Missiological discourse and missional practice necessarily have to take account of the existence (in some sense) of other gods and the phenomenon of idolatry. They are unquestionably something. Yet we are able to engage in such discourse without compromising our fundamental biblical monotheism that there is one and only one living God, known to us in the fullness of his trinitarian revelation. If this were not so, then we would be guilty of implicit polytheism in singing such words as these from a missionary hymn:

> Where other lords beside Thee
> Hold their unhindered sway,
> Where forces that defied Thee
> Defy Thee still today.[7]

We can sing such words, of course, in full assurance of Paul's affirmation (which, we remember, was based on Deuteronomy and, apart from its christological claim, expressed a paradox that Deuteronomy would have understood and accepted) that although there are many gods and lords in the world, there is in reality only one Lord and one God, from whom and for whom all things exist. If *we* can sing such words and engage in the kind of theological discourse that underlies them, without thereby placing ourselves at some inferior stage of religious evolution that falls short of true monotheism, I can see no reason why it is necessary to place an ancient Israelite in some such artificial location when he or she also sang, or prophesied, or legislated, making reference to other gods that held sway over the nations or defied Yahweh, the one living God.

To conclude this opening discussion: Are the gods we meet in the Bible something or nothing? The paradoxical answer is that they are both. On the one hand, they are nothing in comparison with Yahweh, the one true living God. They do not have any divine existence like his, for he alone occupies that transcendent realm of deity. Yahweh alone is God, *and there is no other*. Yet, on the other hand, the gods were clearly something within the world of the peoples and cultures that named them, worshiped them, subjected themselves to them, or enlisted them in whatever objectives were being pursued by the powerful among men for their own ends. So what is that something? What are the gods?

CHAPTER TWO

WHAT ARE THE GODS?

So THEN, IF THE GODS are not *God in the way Yahweh alone is God* and yet exist as something, what are they? If they do not exist within the realm of true divinity (the realm in which Yahweh is the sole and exclusive incumbent), then they must exist within the only other realm of being—the created order. If they are created entities, they must exist either within the world of the *physical* creation (which subdivides into the natural order created by God and the products of human manufacture) or in the *invisible* world of the nonhuman spirits also created by God. The Bible offers us all three as ways of categorizing the something of idolatry. Idols and gods may be (1) objects within the visible creation, (2) demons, and (3) the product of human hands. Let us look at each of these.

Idols and gods as objects within creation

In the physical creation, it was well observed in Israel that some people regarded the heavenly bodies as gods and worshiped them, while others did the same to creatures on the earth, whether nonhuman animals, or even fellow human beings. All of these, of course, since they are created by the living God, should not in themselves be objects of worship. The warning given against such deification of the created order in Deuteronomy 4:15-21 interestingly (and almost certainly deliberately) lists the objects thus worshiped in directly opposite order to their creation in Genesis 1: humans, male and female; land animals; birds of the air; fish in the waters; sun, moon, and stars. The rhetorical effect of this inversion matches the theological implication: when people worship creation instead of the Creator, everything is turned upside down. Idolatry produces disorder in all our fundamental relationships. Idolatry is life lived in a topsy-turvy universe that denies and discombobulates God's created order.

Worship of the heavenly bodies was as ancient as it was widespread but was inconsistent with Israel's faith in Yahweh as Creator. Thus even in the mouth of Job (who is not described as an Israelite but is commended by the narrator and by Yahweh himself as a devout worshiper of God), it is rejected as sin and unfaithfulness.

> If I have regarded the sun in its radiance
>   or the moon moving in splendor,
> so that my heart was secretly enticed
>   and my hand offered them a kiss of homage,
> then these also would be sins to be judged,
>   for I would have been unfaithful to God on high.
>   (Job 31:26-28)

Nevertheless, astral worship clearly infected Israel badly at times (see, e.g., Amos 5:26; 2 Kings 17:16; 21:3-5; Ezek 8:16). In Isaiah 40:26 the prophet invites the exiles, who were probably dazzled by the apparent power of these star gods of their Babylonian conquerors, to look up to the heavens. Then he simply asks the question, "Who created all these?" The very question unmasks them. The stars are not all-powerful gods controlling the destinies of nations. They are not even gods at all. They are merely creatures of the living God, summoned and controlled by his authority.

Worship of the nonhuman animal creation is also common, and in ancient Israel's context was particularly associated with Egypt, where a variety of animals and reptiles were deified (see Ezek 24:9-11).

Idols and gods as demons

Turning to the nonphysical created order, Israel was well aware of the hosts of heaven, the spiritual beings that surround the seat of God's supreme government, serve God's purposes, and do God's bidding. Mostly. For Israel was also aware (though it gave the matter less theological reflection) of agencies within that exalted company that *questioned* God (as did "the satan," or the accuser, in Job 1), or *challenged* God's truthfulness and benevolence (as did the serpent, whatever it represents, in Gen 3), or *accused* God's servants (as the satan does to Joshua, the postexilic high priest, in Zech 3:1-2). Such spirits, however they were envisaged, remain entirely subject to Yahweh's authority, so that even a "lying spirit" can be dispatched to serve the purpose of Yahweh's intended judgment on Ahab (1 Kings 22:19-23).

Only rarely do Old Testament texts connect the worship of other gods with demons, but the rarity should not lead us to overlook that the connection was made, for it was certainly picked up and amplified theologically in the New Testament. Thus, for example, it is an assumption made by Paul, doubtless with what he regarded as scriptural legitimacy, that flirting with idols could lead to participation with demons (1 Cor 10:18-21). Gordon Fee notes:

> Although the Old Testament itself contains no theological reflection on this understanding of idolatry (that is, as the worship of demons), it was the natural development of Israel's realisation that the "mute" gods of the pagans did in fact have supernatural powers. Since there was only one God, such power could not be attributed to a god; hence the belief arose that idols represented demonic spirits.[1]

The connection seems to have been made at an early stage, since the first text specifically to speak of other gods as demons is the Song of Moses in Deuteronomy 32, which is acknowledged by many scholars to be very early Israelite poetry.

> They made him jealous with their foreign gods
>   and angered him with their detestable idols.

> They sacrificed to demons,[2] which are not God. (Deut 32:16-17,
>   altered slightly; see also Deut 32:21, NIV false gods)

Psalm 106 has a similar purpose to Deuteronomy 32. Its primary focus
is on the sin of idolatry. First the idolatry of the golden bull calf at Mount
Sinai is mentioned (Ps 106:19-20—in a wonderfully sarcastic contrast
between Yahweh as the Glory of Israel and "an image of a bull, which
eats grass"!). Then, second, the terrible apostasy at Baal Peor is recalled,
where the gods are described as "dead things" (Ps 106:28, lit. "they ate
sacrifices of dead ones/things"; NIV "lifeless gods"). Finally, in the land
itself, Israel, against all instructions, followed the cultic practices of the
Canaanites (lit. "learned their doings").

> They mingled with the nations
>   and adopted their customs.
> They worshiped their idols,
>   which became a snare to them.
> They sacrificed their sons
>   and their daughters *to demons* [NIV false gods].
> They shed innocent blood,
>   the blood of their sons and daughters,
>   whom they sacrificed to the idols of Canaan,
>   and the land was desecrated by their blood. (Ps 106:35-38)

These texts (Deut 32; Ps 106) are the only two Old Testament passages
that clearly and explicitly equate gods and idols with demons, though
there are hints elsewhere.[3] However, they certainly do provide scriptural
foundation for Paul's blunt assertion that "the sacrifices of pagans are offered to demons, not to God" (1 Cor 10:20). This conviction is of a piece
with Paul's theological assessment of idolatry elsewhere. In what was
probably his earliest letter Paul recalls how the Thessalonians "turned to
God from idols to serve the living and true God" (1 Thess 1:9)—"the clear
implication being that their former worship of idols had been the worship
of dead and false gods," as Brian Wintle puts it.[4] In Luke's record of Paul's
description before Agrippa of his encounter with the risen Jesus, Paul

deems this turning from idols as tantamount to being released from the power of Satan (Acts 26:18). Conversely, the book of Revelation portrays the finally impenitent and rebellious as those who, even after the initial manifestations of God's judgment, refuse to turn from their idolatry, which is then described as follows: "[they] did not repent of the work of their hands; they did not stop worshiping demons, and idols of gold, silver, bronze, stone and wood—idols that cannot see or hear or walk" (Rev 9:20).

The connection is clear: to worship other gods is to worship satanic demons that infest the very statues that represent them.

Idols and gods as the work of human hands

Returning to the Old Testament, if the description of gods and idols as *demons* is rare, the description that Revelation 9:20 pairs with it, "the work of their hands," is pervasive and typical. Indeed, second only to the fact that idolatry is fundamentally rebellion against the living God, this is probably the major basis of the critique of idolatry in the Old Testament. Idols and gods are human constructs! An idol is not even a *living* creature in its own right but merely the *manufacture* of a creature. What possible claim can it have to be divine?

We need to take this biblical perception seriously and to sample the strength of this charge in some representative Old Testament texts. The expression "fashioned by human hands" (*ma ʿăśēh yədê- ʾādām*) is disparagingly applied to other gods a number of times. Hezekiah, for example, is not surprised that the Assyrians had been able to defeat other nations and at the same time destroy their gods. This was the point that the Assyrian general, Rabshakeh, had hoped would persuade Hezekiah that his own little god Yahweh would fare no differently. Hezekiah knew his God better. So he prayed for deliverance so that the rest of the world might know better too (an interesting missional perspective in itself). Thus Hezekiah comments in his prayer:

> It is true, LORD, that the Assyrian kings have laid waste these nations and their lands. They have thrown their gods into the fire and destroyed them, for they were not gods [or not God], but only

wood and stone, fashioned by human hands. Now, LORD our God, deliver us from his hand, so that all kingdoms of the earth may know that you alone, LORD, are God. (2 Kings 19:17-19)[5]

Psalmists also joined the contempt.

> Their idols are silver and gold,
>   made by human hands.
> They have mouths, but cannot speak,
>   eyes, but cannot see.
> They have ears, but cannot hear,
>   noses, but cannot smell.
> They have hands, but cannot feel,
>   feet, but cannot walk;
>   nor can they utter a sound with their throats.
> Those who make them will be like them,
>   and so will all who trust in them. (Ps 115:4-8;
>   see Ps 135:15-18)

Prophets, as one would expect, adopt the same rhetorical polemic.

> With their silver and gold
>   they make idols for themselves
>   to their own destruction. . . .
> This calf—a metalworker has made it;
>   it is not God. (Hos 8:4, 6)

> They make idols for themselves from their silver,
> cleverly fashioned images,
>   all of them the work of craftsmen. (Hos 13:2)

> Of what value is an idol carved by a craftsman?
>   Or an image that teaches lies?
> For the one who makes it trusts in his own creation;
>   he makes idols that cannot speak.
> Woe to him who says to wood, "Come to life!"
>   Or to lifeless stone, "Wake up!"

Can it give guidance?
It is covered with gold and silver;
there is no breath in it. (Hab 2:18-19)

These sharp challenges are surpassed in rhetorical and descriptive force only by the other two great prophetic texts that highlight the human origins of idols: Jeremiah 10:3-5, 9, 14 and Isaiah 40:18-20; 44:9-20. These two texts are too long to reproduce, but it really would be worth pausing to read them and feel the full force of both prophets' attack on manmade, handmade idolatry.

Now, it is at this point that ancient Israel is frequently accused by contemporary scholars of religious ignorance and naiveté, in a way that I believe is unfair and needs a robust response.

It is alleged that Israelites regarded all pagan worship as nothing more than fetishism. Israelites mistakenly thought (we are told), that pagan worshipers regarded physical idols as having life and power in themselves. Since they obviously did not, the whole charade was laughable to the Israelites. The Israelites failed to recognize the distinction (which other nations made) between the idols as images, on the one hand, and the gods or heavenly powers that such images represented in the minds and devotions of their worshipers, on the other hand. Committed to aniconic worship themselves (that is, to the worship of Yahweh without images), Israel could not understand or appreciate the subtlety of iconic forms of worship that it saw around it. The real spiritual and psychological dynamic of the use of idols in worship was not grasped by the Israelites, so they simply mocked what they did not understand.

An example of this assumption is found in an otherwise excellent article by John Barton. He argues that from the time of Isaiah,

there develops the tradition of seeing "idols" not as warped representations of the true deity but as images of false gods, and then of identifying the other gods with their images, as if the image were all there was. It has often been noticed that this is in a sense unfair to those who use images in worship. The iconoclast

[Israelite] sees only the image and thinks that the worshipper who uses it is bowing down before a mere physical object. But this is the iconoclast's interpretation of what the worshipper is doing. For the worshipper the image is a representation of a divine power, which is not exhausted by the image but somehow symbolized by or encapsulated in it. Nevertheless this "unfair" interpretation of idols established itself as the main line of thinking about images in the pages of the Old Testament.[6]

So runs the argument, usually with the moral that we should avoid falling into the same ignorant condemnation of those whose objects or forms of worship differ from our own. It is a way of neutralizing the Old Testament's condemnation of idolatry that is particularly attractive to advocates of religious pluralism.[7] It is also a way of indulging our own feeling of religious (and moral) superiority to the Old Testament. Since, as a result of modern anthropological research into human religion, we now understand the true spiritual dynamic of what Israel so lamentably ridiculed (we are encouraged to believe), we need not be bound by the narrow and ignorant exclusivism of these polemical texts in the Old Testament. We can be much more indulgent toward those who worship idols, for we understand what they are doing in a way that those ignorant Israelites did not.

This widely held assumption, however, seems to me to be even more of a patronizing and unfair misunderstanding of the Israelites than that which it charges against them. For it seems very clear to me that the author of the great polemic against the gods of Babylon understood *precisely* the distinction that was supposed to exist between the physical idols themselves and the gods they represented. So well did he understand the pagan theology on this point, in fact, that he could utilize it in cartoon form to critique idols, gods, and worshipers together. Let us see how.

In Isaiah 46:1-2 the prophet portrays the great Babylonian gods up in heaven, Bel and Nebo. But they are stooping down to earth. Why? Because their idols are in danger of falling off the ox carts on to which they have been loaded. *The prophet understands perfectly well that the statues were not, in Babylonian thinking, the gods themselves.* The gods were invisibly somewhere else "up there." Their statues were visibly "down here." His point is, however, that wherever and whatever those gods may have been thought to be in a Babylonian worldview, when the crunch came they were totally unable to save even their own statues, let alone save their worshipers. On the contrary, the perceived gods became a burden to their worshipers, who felt obliged to try to save their statues by whatever undignified means was available. The gods in the Babylonian heaven had to abandon their statues to the ludicrous insecurity of staggering ox carts on Babylonian streets. The god whose power the statue was supposed to embody or proclaim was actually powerless when his statue needed a hand.

The prophet's satire is not based on naive ignorance but on penetrating insight. In fact, the whole power of his cartoon *presupposes and depends on* his understanding of the Babylonian distinction between images and the gods they stood for. He knew perfectly well that Babylonians distinguished between their idol statues and the gods they visibly depicted. His point is that the manifest failure of alleged gods even to save their own idols was laughably unimpressive. What kind of god was this?

There is evidence also in earlier narrative texts that Israelites were not so obtuse as the pluralist superiority complex wishes to paint them. They perceived that a statue or altar was not in itself the same as the god it was supposed to represent. That did not stop them mocking the impotence of the alleged god, however. Gideon's father, Joash, takes on a hostile crowd after his son has toppled the village altar to Baal and its Asherah pole. Joash nicely distinguishes between the physical symbols of the god and the god himself. His words brilliantly capture the nonsense of a god who needs defending, when one thought that the whole point of having a god was that *he* should defend *you*. At the very least a god should be able to defend his own turf and totem. "Are you going to plead Baal's cause? Are you trying to save him? . . . If Baal really is a god, he can defend himself when someone breaks down his altar" (Judg 6:31).

Baal's tendency to go AWOL when most needed by his worshipers drew even sharper sarcasm from Elijah. Ahab had built an altar for Baal and an Asherah pole. Jezebel had four hundred prophets to serve him. But wherever Baal was in spiritual reality, he was not around at the altar of his demented devotees on Mount Carmel. Elijah's mockery is an ad hominem argument addressed to their assumption that he *is* a god, after all, so he must be somewhere else, if not here. Elijah knew perfectly well that the assumed god Baal was not the same thing as whatever objects represented him on earth. "'Shout louder!' he said. 'Surely he is a god! Perhaps he is deep in thought, or busy, or traveling. Maybe he is sleeping and must be awakened'" (1 Kings 18:27).

This brings us back to our main point. The Israelites, then, fully aware of what *idols* were supposed to signify among those who bowed down before them, nevertheless castigated them as the work of human hands. What, then, did this signify for the *gods* that the idols represented? The radical conclusion has to be that the psalmists and prophets make no distinction between the images and the gods they represented—*not because they did not know that such a distinction was there in the minds of pagan worshipers, but because ultimately there was no such distinction in reality.*

The *visible idols* were obviously manmade. Anybody could see that. But also, and here is the point, whatever the *invisible gods* might be thought to be (by their own worshipers or by Israelites tempted to join them), *they too were nothing more than human constructs.* The alleged gods that the idols represented had no *divine* reality or *divine* power, for such reality and power belonged to Yahweh alone. That the gods, in the myths and cult of their worshipers, were thought to inhabit some other sphere generally invisible to humans made no difference to their actual status as the product of human imagination. Mere invisibility was no proof of divinity.

So, in declaring the idols, which everybody could see had been manufactured by human effort and skill, to be the work of human hands, the Israelites were doing much more than merely stating the obvious. After all, the pagan worshipers would have agreed on that point. *Of course* idol statues were the work of human hands in pagan minds! Not only did everybody know that, but they actually *prided* themselves on the skill and expense that their hands put into making those great images (as is still true in countries, such as India, where idols are an important part of popular religion). Rather, the Israelite theologians were *including* in that "handmade" assessment not only the idols but also all that the idols were believed by their worshipers to stand for—the alleged gods as well. *The gods "in heaven," too, were just as manmade as their all too obviously manmade statues on earth.*

John Barton, in the thoughtful article mentioned above, sees Isaiah as the one to whom Israel owed this breakthrough realization about the gods, that they were not in reality alternative sources of *divine* power, but merely human products.

> [Isaiah] departs from the idea that other gods are an alternative source of divine power, distinct from Yahweh, and presents them instead as products of human devising. Whereas for Hosea it is wrong to seek alliances with other nations because this involves getting entangled with their gods, who are threatening alternative sources of divine power forbidden to the Israelites, Isaiah regards trust in foreign nations as trust in merely human sources of strength. "The Egyptians are human, and not God; their horses are flesh, and not spirit" (Isa 31:3). The gods of other nations are similarly not gods at all, but human fictions: they are manmade and can be described as "the work of their hands" (2:8). To rely on a foreign god is not to rely on another [divine] source of strength, not even one which is forbidden, but to rely on something which human beings have devised and which is therefore no stronger than they are. Thus there is no talk of cultic *apostasy* in Isaiah in the sense of abandoning Yahweh for other gods who are real, but more of cultic *stupidity*, worshipping as a divine source of strength something that is no more powerful than the worshippers themselves.[8]

In my view, Barton is absolutely right here, and has perceived something quite radical and profound in Israel's assessment of idolatry, something that has far-reaching missiological significance.[9]

Those gods that people worship, other than the one living God, are something within the created order, with no objective divine reality. When they are not objects within the physical creation (such as the sun and stars, or living creatures), when they are not demons or spirits of some kind, then they must be (and are most commonly described as) "the work of human hands." *The alleged gods are in fact no different from the idols that represent them; they are both human constructs.* In worshiping them, we give allegiance to—we attribute power and authority to, we submit ourselves to—something that we ourselves have created. In the final analysis, the satire of Isaiah 44:9-20 is not off the mark. There is *in principle* no difference between the domestic fetishist and the sophisticated iconic worshiper of the great gods of Babylon. Whether addressing the piece of wood he has carved for himself as if it were actually a god (Is 44:17) or calling out to the invisible state gods supposedly represented in the gilded statues (Is 46:7), the worshiper is engaged in an exercise in futility. The one is as much the product of collective human imagination as the other is the work of individual human hands. There is no salvation in either.

Significantly, most of the references to gods and idols being the work of human hands occur in contexts where it is particularly national or state gods that are in view. For this is where the power of the gods seems strongest and where Israel's radical assertion is correspondingly most countercultural and polemical. Surely these great national gods of Egypt, Assyria, or Babylon are mighty and powerful divinities? Not so, reply the prophets; they are no more powerful than the people who make them. In making them, of course, the nations have embodied their own pride, greed, and aggression.

This is a strong biblical anticipation of a contemporary phenomenon to which we shall give attention in part two. Pride, greed, and aggression, in the forms of nationalism, consumerism, and militarism, still elevate themselves into idolatrous status in our modern Western cultures. The old gods may have changed their names or lost their personal names altogether in favor of more abstract concepts and phrases (patriotism, the free market, economic growth, national security, etc.), but they can still wield enormous power in the popular mindset—power we ourselves give to them as deified human constructs. They still tend to solidify and justify the power of the powerful and the wealth of the wealthy—and the sacrifices of the rest, which all false gods demand.

National gods, then, both ancient and modern, are the ultimate deification of human pride, but they remain human constructs nevertheless.

For what did it actually mean to say that the great gods of Assyria had defeated the lesser gods of the smaller nations around Judah, for example? Only that the Assyrian king and his armies had rampaged through those countries with vicious cruelty and greed (Is 10:12-14). Indeed, that was the explanation given by the Assyrian king and his spokesman themselves (2 Kings 18:33-35). Within their worldview, what happened in the sphere of kings and armies reflected what was going on in the sphere of the gods. So there was no difficulty for a king to claim to have defeated gods. Kings and gods could be interchangeable in grammar or on the ground.

The Israelite prophets accepted this worldview at one level but decisively rejected it at another. The international *human* arena was indeed the sphere of *divine* action (that was the part they agreed on). But far from it being an arena packed with clashing gods (that was the part they rejected), only one divine being was active within it—Yahweh the God of Israel, about whom Hezekiah could say, "You alone are God over all the kingdoms of the earth. You have made heaven and earth" (2 Kings 19:15). The gods to which the Assyrians attributed their military victory, just as much as the gods of the nations they had pillaged, were "not gods" or "not God"—that is, they had no share in the sovereign divine reality that belonged to Yahweh alone—but were only "fashioned by human hands" (2 Kings 19:18).

Habakkuk makes the same assertion. Having described in graphic detail the arrogance, the violence, the human *and environmental* destructiveness of Assyria's imperial expansion (Hab 2:3-17), he scoffs at the idea that their gods could provide any defense against the doom that is coming to them from the hand of the Lord. That is the context of the following verses, and the point of their scorn, which is followed by the customary mockery of wood and stone, decked out in silver and gold but devoid of life and breath:

> Of what value is an idol carved by a craftsman?
>> Or an image that teaches lies?
> For *the one who makes it trusts in his own creation;*
>> he makes idols that cannot speak. (Hab 2:18 emphasis added)

There could hardly be a clearer articulation of exactly what Israel's prophets believed about the great state gods of their imperial enemies than that single line: "the one who makes it trusts in his own creation" (lit. "the maker of the thing he has made trusts in it"). There is no divine power in or behind or above the idols. They are not icons of *deity* but fictions of *humanity.* By contrast, Habakkuk goes on, "The LORD is in his holy temple; let all the earth [not just Israel] be silent before him" (Hab 2:20).

If this was true for the Assyrian idol worshipers themselves (that their gods were the work of human hands), then the same shattering exposure could be aimed at those *Israelites* who opted to worship the gods of Assyria. Thus, when Hosea writes a liturgy of repentance (sadly never used) for the people of Israel, he tells them that what they need to do is to recognize the impotence of the Assyrian military machine to save them, *precisely because* their trust in it is nothing more than trusting in gods *their own hands* have made. In other words, the power that Assyria's gods seemed to exercise over Israel was as much the product of *Israel's* imagination as of the Assyrians' religion. To worship those gods was to connive in the attribution of divinity to what was a human construct. It was to take into your own imagination the human constructions of the enemy and submit to them. So to *repent* of trusting in Assyria's armed forces (and thereby trusting in Assyrian gods) was to repent of having *made gods for themselves.*

> Take words with you
>> and return to the LORD.

Say to him:
  "Forgive all our sins
and receive us graciously,
    that we may offer the fruit of our lips.
Assyria cannot save us;
  we will not mount *warhorses.*
We will never again say '*Our gods*'
    to *what our own hands have made.*" (Hos 14:2-3
      emphasis added)

Hosea preached to the northern kingdom of Israel. There is great irony in telling them that in going after the gods of *Assyria* they were trusting in gods of their own manufacture, since the founding king of Israel, Jeroboam I, had effectively done the same thing to Yahweh himself and for the same reason—to bolster the security of his new and vulnerable state. First Kings 12:26-33 shows both the motivation and the subtlety of his actions.

Jeroboam's intention was to prevent his population reverting to political allegiance to Jerusalem through religious pilgrimage to Yahweh's temple there. So he provided calf images at opposite ends of his kingdom as places for the northern tribes to worship the God who had brought them up out of Egypt. Clearly he did not want to be seen to be suggesting the worship of any other god but Yahweh, and indeed the text hints that Jeroboam may have been claiming the mantle of Moses in having delivered the tribes from the oppression of Solomon and son. Nevertheless, he reconstructed the whole religious apparatus of his state so that the cult of Yahweh was clearly under his patronage.[10] So the narrative subtly implies that while the name at the top of the page was still Yahweh, the table of contents was very much of Jeroboam's own making. Yahweh himself had now been fashioned like a god made by human hands. Yahweh, as used by Jeroboam, became a human construct for political purposes, including (most probably) national security.

The living God, then, was being commandeered and crafted through state propaganda to serve the needs of national security—a form of idolatry that did not perish with Jeroboam, as we will explore in part two. One of the horrendous blasphemies of the modern West has been the ease of using the name of God in association with national aggrandization. It is well known that both major protagonists in the cataclysmic destruction of the First World War claimed "God is on our side." Genocides in South Africa, North America, and Australia have been given theological divine sanction. "One nation under God" and "In God we trust" are relatively recent inventions giving somewhat ironic expression to American identity and setting religiously sanctioned capitalism against atheistic communism. "For God and Ulster" was paraded on banners that I remember in my homeland, Northern Ireland, to bolster the tribal identity and political hegemony of Protestants.

Moving back from the prophets to Psalm 115, the psalm that most sharply declares the human origin of idols, it is noticeable again that the polemical context is between Israel and the nations. The familiar opening verse of the psalm also takes on greater significance in the light of our discussion thus far. If the gods of a nation are in fact the collective human construct of that nation's pride, then the glory of a god is identical to the glory of its nation and vice versa. To glorify a nation's *god* usually meant praising that nation's *military might*. The Israelite psalmist denies that this can be any part of the motivation for praising Yahweh the God of Israel. On the contrary, he says, with double emphasis, "Not to us, LORD, not to us but to your name be the glory, because of your love and faithfulness" (Ps 115:1).

That is to say, to give glory to *Yahweh* must never be construed as just another way of giving glory to his people *Israel*. On the contrary, Yahweh must be praised for his own distinct identity and character, not just as a symbol or cipher for the people's own self-congratulation (a confusion that is as seductive as it is rampant among modern nations that claim to honor "God" in national ceremonies, or sloganize a pious-sounding "God bless America" in otherwise blatantly political speeches).

The worst manifestation of gods as the work of human hands is when humans claim to be their own gods or to be the divine source of their own power. The quip about "the self-made man who worships his creator" is recognized in the Old Testament, and even comes in for the same kind of grim humor in the process of unmasking the absurdity and deception of such arrogance. Yet again, it is usually the vice of kings and emperors.

Ezekiel exposes the self-divination of the king of Tyre and the inevitable judgment it brings on him and his empire:

> In the pride of your heart
>   you say, "I am a god;
> I sit on the throne of a god
>   in the heart of the seas."
> But you are a mere mortal and not a god,
>   though you think you are as wise as a god. . . .
> Will you then say, "I am a god,"
>   in the presence of those who kill you?
> You will be but a mortal, not a god,
>   in the hands of those who slay you. (Ezek 28:2, 9)

Similarly, Ezekiel pointedly expresses the arrogance of the pharaoh of Egypt who imagines himself to be the source of his own prosperity, claiming the divine power of creation over the Nile that itself provides the wealth of Egypt.

> I am against you, Pharaoh king of Egypt,
>   you great monster lying among your streams.
> You say, "The Nile belongs to me;
>   I made it for myself." (Ezek 29:3)

What insane arrogance and self-deception fuel such an absurd claim! Yet it is echoed in the idolatrous worship of Mammon that characterizes contemporary global capitalism. Is there not an ugly irony in the self-styled and semiblasphemous "masters of the universe" as a term for those making massive and almost instant fortunes in clever deals in the financial markets? It is also evident in the way individuals who have accumulated vast amounts of wealth in business (with or without effective scrutiny) are lauded as assumed experts in other quite unrelated fields of human interaction—politics, for example. Mammon rules in both spheres, as the extent of corruption by corporate lobbying and the eye-watering scale of money spent on getting elected (or not) exposes. We seem content to be ruled by the "best" government money can buy. Even megachurch pastors whose wealth may have come from spiritually dubious sources are "idolized" as celebrities of great wisdom and their published words revered like Delphi oracles of old.

God is not opposed, of course, to God's own mandate for humans to use the resources of the earth to prosper, trade, and create and share wealth. But when people claim to be the sole source of their own wealth, or indeed the sole owners of the creational resources on which their wealth depends, then God's clear warning pricks the bubble of such pride. "You may say to yourself, 'My power and the strength of my hands have produced this wealth for me.' But remember the LORD your God, for it is he who gives you the ability to produce wealth" (Deut 8:17-18).

When we review the material we have surveyed in this chapter, it is enormously challenging to the whole world of gods and idols, and it was clearly intended to be so. For we have observed this stance across the wide range of Old Testament literature from many different historical periods.

Now, it is not unusual for any people to make great claims for their own deity. In this principle and practice, Israel's exaltation of its god, Yahweh, might be seen as no different from its neighbors.[11] But to claim transcendent uniqueness and universality for that deity, to the exclusion of all others, and to defend the claim by reference to his extraordinary and unparalleled jealousy, as Israel did for Yahweh, was something not found in anything like the same degree elsewhere.

But then to go further still and declare, again and again as a pervasive matter of theological worldview, that the gods of the nations, just as much as the idols that visibly represent them, are "the work of human hands"—human constructs with no divine substance—that is something else and quite unparalleled. Yet there seems no other way to account for the extensiveness of this theme in the Old Testament.

Israel did *not* misunderstand the nature of idolatry or the assumptions that were made by other worshipers about their own gods. On the contrary, understanding those assumptions and claims very well, Israel simply refused to accept them. The categorical assertion of Psalm 96:5 is devastating. "All the gods of the nations are idols [*ĕlîlîm*]"—that is, *the gods themselves* share the same insubstantial transience as the idols, for they are just as manmade.

To say that the gods are work of human hands is to prick human hubris and to invite fierce repudiation. Paul saying it in Ephesus was enough to start a riot (Acts 19:23-41). For if it is indeed true that the gods we exalt so highly are nothing more than the resplendent products of our own creativity, then it is not surprising that we defend them so belligerently. In our own jealous protectiveness of *the gods we create for ourselves*, we parody the true jealousy that is the prerogative of *the only true God whom we did not create*. We invest so much of ourselves in our gods, we spend so much on them, we so deeply blend our identity and significance with theirs, that it simply will not do for us to have them unmasked, mocked, or toppled. Yet, of course, topple they must before the living God. For that is the destiny of all human effort that is not for the glory of God or offered to be redeemed by him.

> Pride of man and earthly glory,
> Sword and crown betray his trust;
> What with care and toil he buildeth,
> Tower and temple fall to dust.
> But God's power,
> Hour by hour,
> Is my temple and my tower.[12]

In the end, the gods of human creation for all their arrogant claims and masquerade are no greater than gilded statues that have to be nailed down to keep them vertical. Against all such pretensions and products of men, Isaiah affirms that

The arrogance of man will be brought low
  and human pride humbled;
the LORD alone will be exalted in that day,
  and the idols will totally disappear. (Is 2:17-18)

Drawing on such scriptural roots, Paul affirms both the created nature of the powers and associated ideologies that hold sway over human lives and minds, and the decisive judgment of all these powers at the cross of Christ: "See to it that no one takes you captive through hollow and deceptive philosophy, which depends on human tradition and the elemental spiritual forces of this world rather than on Christ. . . . Having disarmed the powers and authorities, [Christ] made a public spectacle of them, triumphing over them by the cross" (Col 2:8, 15).

Conclusion

So then, we now have a further paradox about the gods to add to the one we explored in chapter one.

The first paradox as we saw in chapter one is that, on the one hand, the gods are nothing in terms of the divine reality that is claimed for them. There is only one rightful occupant of the category of deity, and that is the Lord God of the biblical revelation, Creator and Ruler of the universe. Yet, on the other hand, idols clearly do exist in our observable world, and the gods they represent also exist within history as part of human discourse, experience, and activity. They are something—something whose existence is assumed in the command not to worship them. The gods exist as somethings, but not as the living God does, with divine identity, status, power, and eternity. By comparison, the gods are nothings.

The second paradox that we have explored in this chapter is that the Old Testament much more frequently and unambiguously describes both idols and the gods they are presumed to represent as the work of human hands. *We are the makers of our own gods*—which, of course, is part of the absurdity of worshiping them.

So if the question is asked, "Are other gods demons or human constructions?" the answer is that they can be either or both. However, the latter is the more significant theological truth and the more dangerous deception. Human beings did not need the devil to teach us idolatry. Once we chose to reject the authority of the living God, we ended up creating gods for ourselves, either within the created order or within the imaginations of our hearts. We are experts in doing so, and the devil fosters our expertise.

If gods are primarily human constructs, then they are our own responsibility. We pay their debts, clear up their mess, suffer their consequences. Certainly we must acknowledge the extent and effect of satanic infiltration and spiritual blindness inflicted by the evil one. But gods and idols are fundamentally what we have made. The secularist accusation against the dire consequences of human religions has some point: the gods we make are as destructive as we are ourselves—for they are the work of our own hands, and our hands are full of blood.

But there is also an element of hope in this awareness. If gods are mainly human constructs, then they are not only destructive, but also *destructible*—just as destructible as anything else we make on earth. *The gods, too, are subject to decay and death.* They are no more durable than the people or empires that make them. The scorn of the Assyrian toward the defunct gods of the nations he had conquered rebounds on himself in the light of history. For where now are the gods of Assyria, or Babylon, or Persia, or Greece, or Rome . . . ?

History is the graveyard of the gods.

CHAPTER THREE

DISCERNING THE GODS

WHY IS IDOLATRY A MISSIONAL ISSUE? Why must mission engage the gods, expose and unmask them? Why must we identify and condemn idolatry (as the prophets and apostles did), not only as it presents itself among those who do not yet acknowledge the living God but also (and even more so) as it works its insidious poison among those who *do* claim to know and worship the God of the Bible and who name the name of Christ (recalling that the prophets condemn idolatry in Israel far more often than in other nations)? What, in any case, is so wrong with people worshiping their own gods if they want to? How are we to recognize the presence of other gods in human cultures, including our own? These are some of the questions to which we turn in this chapter.

Recognizing the most crucial distinction

The most fundamental distinction in all reality is presented to us in the opening verses of the Bible. It is the distinction between the Creator God and everything else that exists anywhere. God alone is uncreated, self-existent, noncontingent. God's being depends on nothing else outside God's own self. All other reality, by contrast, is created by God and therefore is dependent on God for existence and sustenance. The creation is contingent on God. Creation cannot and would not exist without God. God did and could exist without creation. This essential ontological duality between two orders of being (the created order and the uncreated God) is foundational to the biblical worldview.

Flowing from this, there are many other subordinate distinctions within creation itself that the creation narrative alerts us to: the distinctions between day and night, between different environments on earth, between species, between humans in God's image and the rest of the animals, between men and women. But undoubtedly the primary and most crucial distinction is that between the Creator and the creation itself. Not surprisingly, therefore, it is that distinction that comes under attack when the mysterious power of evil makes its appearance in that profoundly simple, yet simply profound, narrative of Genesis 3.

"You will be like God, knowing good and evil," promises the serpent—if only humans would disregard God's boundary markers (Gen 3:5). What could be more plausible or natural for a creature made in the image of God than to want to be "like God"? The key to the temptation seems to be in the second phrase, "knowing good and evil," which I take to imply having moral autonomy. That is, what was being offered by the serpent and then claimed by the human pair through their disobedient act was not just the ability to *recognize* the difference between good and evil (which is surely foundational to any genuine moral freedom or moral capacity and is a faculty commended in the Bible elsewhere) but the right to *define for oneself* good and evil. It is the prerogative of God, in the supreme goodness of his own being, to decide and define what constitutes goodness and therefore conversely what is evil. Humans, however, in choosing to decide for ourselves what *we* will deem good or evil, usurp the prerogative of God in rebellious moral autonomy. At the same time, of course, by making our own definitions in a state of rebellion and disobedience, we end up in the moral perversions and chaos that have pervaded fallen human life ever since.

This interpretation of the phrase is supported by the way God recognizes the nature of what has happened: "The man has now become like one of us, knowing good and evil" (Gen 3:22). God accepts that humans have indeed breached the distinction referred to above. Not that humans have now *become* gods, but that they have chosen to *act as though they were*—defining and deciding for themselves what they will regard as good and evil. Therein lies the root of all other forms of idolatry: we deify our own capacities, and thereby make gods of ourselves, our choices, and all their implications. God then shrinks in horror from the prospect of human immortality and eternal life in such a fallen state and prevents access to the tree of life. God has a better way to bring humanity, redeemed and cleansed, to eternal life.

At the root, then, of all idolatry is human rejection of the God-ness of God and the finality of God's moral authority. The fruit of that basic rebellion is to be seen in many other ways in which idolatry blurs the distinction between God and creation, to the detriment of both.

Idolatry dethrones God and enthrones creation. Idolatry is the attempt to limit, reduce, and control God by refusing his authority, constraining or manipulating his power to act, having him available to serve our interests. At the same time, paradoxically, idolatry exalts things within the created order (whether natural objects in the heavens or on earth, or created spirits, or the products of our own hands or imaginations, as we explored in the previous chapter). Creation is then credited with a potency that belongs only to God; it is sacralized, worshiped, and treated as that from which ultimate meaning can be derived. A great reversal happens: God who should be worshiped becomes an object to be used; creation, which is for our proper use and blessing, becomes the object of our worship.

Once this fundamental distinction is blurred, once this reversal takes place, then devastating personal and social consequences follow. Creation, which derives its own meaning from God, cannot give us in itself the ultimate meaning we crave, so idolatry is doomed to disappointment (to put it at its mildest). Worship of the self eventually implodes in narcissism, nihilism, or sheer amoral selfishness. If nature itself is treated as divine, then all other distinctions begin to be dissolved. There is no difference between human life and all other forms of life. There is no difference between good and evil, since all is ultimately one. So any objective reference point for moral discrimination becomes impossible.

In the light of such confusion, the mission of God is ultimately to restore his whole creation to what it was intended to be—*God's* creation, ruled over by redeemed *humanity*, giving glory and praise to the Creator. Our mission, in participation with that divine mission, and in antici- pation of its final accomplishment, is to work with God in exposing the idols that continue to blur the distinction, and to liberate men and women from the destructive delusions they foster.

Naming the gods

Much helpful work has been done in identifying and analyzing the gods that may be said to dominate modern cultures, especially in Western so- cieties. Some of these studies make extensive use of combined biblical and sociological tools, others less so. Such analyses have powerful mis- siological relevance since they apply this distinctive biblical category (idolatry) to contemporary cultural phenomena, enabling us to see below the surface and recognize idolatrous and/or demonic forces at work. Some of them also are specifically addressed to the missiological question of how we are to expose and confront these cultural idols and to address the liberating message of the biblical gospel to those who are captivated by them. A small sampling of such studies in a footnote must suffice.[1]

Returning, however, to the Bible itself, we find that there are different kinds of gods. That is to say, gods that humans worship other than the living God may be constituted by different things, or may exercise their grip over human lives in different ways. If, as we saw in the last chapter, we are in large measure responsible ourselves as human beings for the gods we create, then it is worth looking at the way the Bible portrays that process. What are the things that we tend to manufacture our gods from?

Things that entice us. "Do not be enticed," warns Deuteronomy 4:19; do not be enticed into worshiping heavenly bodies. The language sug- gests that there are things in creation that are so awe inspiring, so much beyond our reach, our control, or our understanding, that they exercise an enticing attraction to us. This is certainly the flavor of the sin that Job claims to have resisted.

If I have regarded the sun in its radiance
or the moon moving in splendor,

so that my heart was secretly enticed
  and my hand offered them a kiss of homage,
then these also would be sins to be judged,
    for I would have been unfaithful to God on high.
      (Job 31:26-28)

Psalm 96 recognizes the same temptation.

For all the gods of the nations are idols,
  but the LORD made the heavens.
Splendor and majesty are before him;
    strength and glory are in his sanctuary. (Psalm 96:5-6
      emphasis added)

The parallelism and flow of thought between these verses implies that the gods worshiped by the nations are personifications of all that impresses us—splendor and majesty, strength and glory. We look for such magnificence and power, and worship these things wherever they inspire awe and trembling admiration: in the stadiums of great sporting triumph or in the lives of pampered sporting heroes; in massed battalions of soldiers, parades of military hardware, or on the decks of aircraft carriers; on the stage of rock concerts or the glare of TV and movie celebrity; on the pinnacles of the thrusting towers of corporate power and greed in great cities.[2] All of these can be enticing and idolatrous. But such places, says our psalm, are not where you will find genuine deity. If you are looking for true *splendor, majesty, strength, and glory*, they are to be found in the presence of the living Creator God alone. Some commentators see these four words in Psalm 96:6 as personifications, as if they were the great angelic companions of Yahweh's throne, in stark contrast to the false gods that claimed such magnificence but lacked even real existence.[3]

Things we fear. The converse is also true. We turn things that we fear into gods in order to placate them or ward them off by our worship. The psalmist affirms that the Lord "is to be feared above all gods" (Ps 96:4), which suggests that gods other than Yahweh are indeed things that are objects of fear (something, in the paradoxical sense discussed in chap. one). So in the Canaanite pantheon Death (Mot) is a god; the Sea (Yamm), another object of awe and fear, is a god. In other world religions the same phenomenon can be observed—some of the most fearsome faces of evil, anger, vengeance, bloodlust, cruelty, and so on are divinized. Many routine ritual practices, such as avoiding the evil eye, the wearing of protective charms, the use of apotropaic magic and mantras, and so on are manifestations of the deified power of fear. Since there are a great many things in this world for puny human beings to be afraid of, here surely lies one of the roots of polytheistic worldviews. There are as many gods as we have terrors.

It is significant, therefore, that the fear of the Lord plays such a central role in the biblical worldview. It is a potent dimension of radical monotheism that if there is truly only one God, then he alone should be the object of our true fear. Then those who live in the fear of the Lord need live in fear of nothing else. Other objects of fear lose their divine power and their idolatrous grip. This is the testimony of the author of Psalm 34.

> I sought the LORD, and he answered me;
>> he delivered me from all my fears. . . .
> The angel of the LORD encamps around those who fear him,
>> and he delivers them.
>
> Taste and see that the LORD is good;
>> blessed is the man who takes refuge in him.
> Fear the LORD, you his holy people,
>> for those who fear him lack nothing. (Ps 34:4, 7-9)

Or as Nahum Tate puts it, "Fear him, ye saints, and you will then have nothing else to fear."[4]

The idolatrous power of fear is enormous and seems to bear no direct relation to the scale of what is feared. It has been pointed out that although in modern Western society we live lives that are immeasurably safer, healthier, and more free from risk than any previous generation, we are consumed by anxieties, fears, and neuroses. Fed by garish media hype, we swoon at the latest rogue virus and seem willing to spend exorbitant amounts on security measures that can never actually prevent the terror we struggle to fend off.[5] Of course, ever since Pharaoh invoked it to oppress the Hebrews, tyrants (actual or wannabe) know how to exploit the idolatrous power of fear for their own political advantage. A disturbing phenomenon of recent years has been the rise (again) in many countries of "the strong man" political leader, who plays on popular fears (and feeds them with falsehoods) to bolster his own power and control.

Things we trust. Following naturally from the previous point, we tend to idolize the things (or people or systems) in which we place our trust to deliver us from the things we fear. The idolatrous dimension emerges when we place ultimate faith in such things, when we believe all the promises that are made or implied in them, and when we make all the sacrifices that they demand in exchange for what they speciously offer. So whether we aim at financial security to ensure against all future threats, or pour vast quantities of the wealth of the planet and its nations into the gaping maw of military security, or just become personally obsessive about every latest fad that promises immunity from ill health or the wear and tear of physical ageing, these tend to be very costly gods indeed.

The more we trust them the more we spend on them, and vice versa. Since we spend so much on them, we naturally feel cheated when they fail to deliver what we demand in return for our investment. A country can spend billions on star-wars protective systems and then be psychologically devastated and permanently traumatized by a few men who hijack airplanes, wielding knives. The USA spends billions on military and nuclear defense, and then an invisible virus kills more people than all the American soldiers killed in recent wars combined. We load blame and anger on health professionals who have not delivered our entitlement to disease-free virtual immortality. Ultimately we pay the cost of putting ultimate trust in what can never deliver ultimate security. It seems we never learn that false gods never fail to fail. That is the only thing about a false god you can depend on. It will let you down in the end.

By contrast, after magnificent reflections on the sovereign power of the Lord and his word, in redemption, creation, providence, and history, the author of Psalm 33 warns us against investing our hope for salvation anywhere else.

> No king is saved by the size of his army;
>> no warrior escapes by his great strength.
> A horse is a vain hope for deliverance;
>> despite all its great strength it cannot save. (Ps 33:16-17)

Those whose blessing it is to know the Lord know that the only secure place to deposit one's investment of trust is in the Lord himself, and then to wait in hope, joy, and patience for the outcome of his *unfailing* love.

> We wait in hope for the LORD;
>> he is our help and shield.
> In him our hearts rejoice,
>> for we trust in his holy name.
> May your unfailing love be with us, LORD,
>> even as we put our hope in you. (Ps 33:20-22)

Things we need. "Do not worry, saying, 'What shall we eat?' or 'What shall we drink?' or 'What shall we wear?' For the pagans run after all these things, and your heavenly Father knows that you need them" (Mt 6:31-32). The words of Jesus acknowledge not only the reality of basic human needs but also the way that "pagans run after" them. We are, of course, creatures with the same fundamental needs as the rest of the animals. Like other mammals, we humans need food, air, water, shelter, sleep, and all the general necessities of survival and welfare. There is, therefore, a natural tendency to deify the sources from which these necessities are deemed to come. Having turned our back on the sole living Creator of all that provides for our needs, we invent surrogate deities to fill the vacuum. So we attribute the varied good gifts of our one

Creator to the varied gods of the rain, of the sun, of the soil, of sex and fertility, of dreams, and so on. Much religious effort is then directed at persuading these gods to bestow their largesse in a way that meets human basic needs, or to reverse their apparent decision to withhold their favor. The behavior of the prophets of Baal who fell under Elijah's mockery, in their desperate attempts to persuade Baal to demonstrate his deity, was probably not untypical in such emergencies.

This was part of the burden of Hosea's accusation against Israel—that it was attributing to Baal and the Canaanite cults all the natural processes and products that were the gift of Yahweh alone (Hos 2:5-8). But this feature of idolatry also gives a sharper polemical edge to the emphatic insistence in Israel's worship on acknowledging Yahweh alone as the source of all that we need. No other god is to be asked for what we need or thanked when we receive it.

> You care for the land and water it;
>> you enrich it abundantly.
> The streams of God are filled with water
>> to provide the people with grain,
>> for so you have ordained it. (Ps 65:9)

> He makes grass grow for the cattle,
>> and plants for people to cultivate—
>> bringing forth food from the earth:
> wine that gladdens human hearts,
>> oil to make their faces shine,
>> and bread that sustains their hearts. (Ps 104:14-15)

Deuteronomy 8 exposes another subtle form of this idolatry of need. Failure to acknowledge the living God as the source of all that provides for our needs and contributes to our flourishing can lead to the arrogance that attributes all that provision to our own strength and effort. This is also a form of idolatry—the worship of oneself as the source of all that meets one's own needs. Whether the Israelite farmer (or the modern capitalist) who boasts, "My power and the strength of my hands have produced this wealth for me" (Deut 8:17), or the Egyptian Pharaoh (or modern economic superpower) who boasts, "The Nile belongs to me; I made it for myself" (Ezek 29:3), both must recognize the idolatrous nature (and insane arrogance) of such claims and acknowledge the true source of the blessings they enjoy.

A missiological perspective on idolatry, then, must include some analysis of the roots of the gods we make for ourselves. Our reflections above suggest some of the ways the Bible itself analyzes what lies behind the things we idolize.

- Having alienated ourselves from the living God our Creator, we have a tendency to worship whatever makes us tremble with awe as we feel our tiny insignificance in comparison with the great magnitudes that surround us.
- We seek to placate and ward off whatever makes us vulnerable and afraid.
- We then counter our fears by investing inordinate and idolatrous trust in whatever we think will give us the ultimate security we crave.
- We struggle to manipulate and persuade whatever we believe will provide all our basic needs and enable us to prosper on the planet.

Doubtless there are other sources and motivations for endemic human idolatry, but these seem to be some of the primary ones, both observed in the Bible and evident to any observer of contemporary human cultures (whether predominantly religious or "secular"). All of them stem from our basic rejection of the living Creator God, before whom all such considerations either evaporate or find their subordinate level of legitimacy.

The only antidote to such idolatries, and therefore the task of biblical mission, is to lead people back to acknowledge the only true and living God in all of these domains. Reviewing our list of the sources of idolatry once more, by way of contrast:

- The one who has set his glory above the heavens is the only one before whom we should tremble in awe and worship.

- To live in covenantal fear of the Lord as sovereign Creator and gracious Redeemer is to be delivered from the fear of anything else in all creation—material or spiritual.
- As the Rock, he is the utterly secure place to invest all our trust in all the circumstances of life and death, for the present and the future.
- As he is the Provider of all that is needful for all life on earth, the God of the covenant with Noah and our heavenly Father, there is no other to whom we need turn, to plead, placate, or persuade, for the needs he already knows we have.

Exposing the gods

We have already reflected more than once on the impotence of the gods of human manufacture. False gods fail. That is their only truth. Since the task of mission involves the exposure of false gods, it is worth exploring in more detail some dimensions of this failure. For although false gods never fail to fail, it seems humans never fail to forget. Some of the accusations that the Bible lays against idolatry include the following:

Idols deprive God of his proper glory. When human beings attribute to other gods the gifts, powers, or functions that belong to the one living God, then God is deprived of the honor that is due to his name alone. The whole creation exists for the glory of the Creator, and in rendering praise to God alone creation (including humanity) experiences its own true blessing and good. This is the meaning of the jealousy of Yahweh in the Old Testament. It is God's proper protection of God's own identity and transcendent uniqueness. "I am the LORD; that is my name! I will not yield my glory to another or my praise to idols" (Is 42:8).

Accordingly, the psalmist, having denounced all the gods of the nations as nothings (in Ps 96:5), issues the universal summons:

Ascribe to *the* LORD, all you families of nations,
    ascribe to *the* LORD glory and strength.
Ascribe to the LORD the glory due *his* name;
    bring an offering and come into *his* courts.

> Worship the LORD in the splendor of *his* holiness;
>> tremble before *him*, all the earth. (Ps 96:7-9 italics intended
>> to emphasize the implied contrast)

This is not an invitation to the nations to make room for Yahweh among the pantheon of their own gods and give him some shared respect. The psalmist is not inviting the nations to move their gods along the shelf a little to make room for Yahweh among their number. No, this is a call for the radical displacement of all other gods before the sole, unique, transcendent God-ness of Yahweh, such that all honor, glory, worship, and praise goes to him, as it rightfully should. As long as other gods are worshiped, the living God is to that extent denied what is rightfully his—the total worship of his total creation. This is what makes the struggle with idolatry a major dimension of the mission of God, in which he commands our cooperation.

Idols distort the image of God in human beings. Since idolatry diminishes the glory of God, and since humans are made in the image of God, it follows that idolatry is also detrimental to the very essence of our humanity. As the Shorter Catechism of the Westminster Confession reminds us, "Man's chief end is to glorify God and enjoy him forever." To refuse to glorify God, and even worse, to exchange "the glory of the immortal God for images made to look like a mortal human being and birds and animals and reptiles" (Rom 1:23), is to frustrate the purpose of our very existence. *Idolatry is radical self-harm.*

It is also radically, terribly ironic. In trying to be as God (in the original temptation and rebellion), we have ended up becoming *less* human. The principle is affirmed in several places in the Bible that you become like the object of your worship (e.g., Ps 115:8; Is 41:24; 44:9). If you worship that which is not *God*, you reduce the image of God in yourself. If you worship that which is not even *human*, you reduce your humanity still further.

So, Isaiah 44 holds before us very starkly the irony (or parody) of the one creature on earth that was made in the image of the living God (a human being) worshiping something that is merely a lifeless image of himself.

The blacksmith takes a tool
    and works with it in the coals;
he shapes an idol with hammers,
    he forges it with the might of his arm.
He gets hungry and loses his strength;
    he drinks no water and grows faint.
The carpenter measures with a line
    and makes an outline with a marker;
he roughs it out with chisels
    and marks it with compasses.
He shapes it *in human form,*
    human form in all its glory,
    that it may dwell in a shrine. (Is 44:12-13 emphasis added)

The words in italics are surely the climax of the prophet's satire. "Human form in all its glory" speaks of the human privilege of being made in the image of God. Yet here is a man worshiping as a god something that is nothing but an image of himself, the product of human skill and effort. The lifeless image of the living man languishes inside a little hut, while the living image of the living God is walking around outside, oblivious to the irony of his actions.

There is comparable (though perhaps more polite) irony also in Paul's argument with the Greek intelligentsia in Athens. Few cultures have equaled ancient Greece in exalting the human spirit, human art, literature, philosophy—even the human physical form. Yet in the process they had lost the very God in whose image all these wonderful dimensions of humanity have their source. Is it not absurd, Paul challenges them, to imagine that the one who is the *origin* of all this human glory needs to be housed and fed by human hands?

The God who made the world and everything in it is the Lord of heaven and earth and does not live in temples built by human hands. And he is not served by human hands, as if he needed anything. Rather, he himself gives everyone life and breath and everything else. . . .

Therefore since we are God's offspring, we should not think that
the divine being is like gold or silver or stone—an image made by
human design and skill. (Acts 17:24-25, 29)

The psalms similarly play on the contrast between the work of God's
hands and the work of human hands. Human beings, like all the rest of
creation, are the work of God's hands (Ps 138:8; 139:13-15). Yet we,
unique among God's creatures, have been made "ruler over the works of
your hands" (Ps 8:6). When one thinks about that in the light of contemplating the vastness of the heavens, which are also "the work of your
fingers," it is astonishing (Ps 8:3). What a travesty it is when humans,
who themselves are the work of God's hands and were made to rule the
rest of the works of God's hands, choose instead to worship the work of
their own hands (Ps 115:4). Without doubt, idolatry distorts, demeans,
and diminishes our humanity.

Idols are profoundly disappointing. In a polytheistic universe, you
cannot expect all the gods to please all the people all the time. So disappointment with the gods is part of the lottery of life. Spread your bets
among the gods, then. You win some, you lose some. The assumption
that some of the gods will disappoint you some of the time is actually
built into such a worldview and becomes inevitable when the conflicts
of the nations are seen as mirroring the conflicts of the gods. Defeated
nations have defeated gods. Threatened nations should face the like-
lihood of their gods failing them too. Best not to trust the same old gods
too long. Switch to the gods of the winning side and avoid disappointment. The gods compete for human loyalty, because, as in all com-
petition, there are going to be losers.

This is precisely the assumption that seemed gloatingly self-
evident to the Assyrian commander swaggering below the walls of
besieged Jerusalem.

Do not listen to Hezekiah, for he is misleading you when he says,
"The LORD will deliver us." Has the god of any nation ever delivered his land from the hand of the king of Assyria? Where are

the gods of Hamath and Arpad? Where are the gods of Sepharvaim, Hena and Ivvah? Have they rescued Samaria from my hand? Who of all the gods of these countries has been able to save his land from me? How then can the LORD deliver Jerusalem from my hand? (2 Kings 18:32-35)

In other words, reasoned the Assyrian, Yahweh would turn out to be as big a disappointment to the people of Judah as the gods of the other nations had been to the Assyrians. From where he stood, that seemed a solid, predictable bet. You just can't trust these lesser gods, you see. Give them up while you can. Join the winners.

Hezekiah and Isaiah, however, had a rather different perspective on events. On the one hand, Hezekiah knew that the reason the other gods had disappointed the nations that trusted in them was that "they were not gods [or not God] but only wood and stone, fashioned by human hands" (2 Kings 19:18). On the other hand, Isaiah knew that Assyria's victories, far from proving the superiority of Assyrian gods, were actually planned and controlled by Yahweh all along, and would very soon be reversed in the fires of his judgment (2 Kings 19:25-28).

No wonder, then, that the same prophet ridiculed Judah for turning away from the only source of protection that would *not* disappoint it to the armies, horses, and gods of the Egyptians, who were notoriously untrustworthy and undoubtedly *would* disappoint them.

Woe . . . to those . . .
who go down to Egypt
    without consulting me;
who look for help to Pharaoh's protection,
    to Egypt's shade for refuge.
But Pharaoh's protection will be to your shame,
    Egypt's shade will bring you disgrace. . . .
But the Egyptians are mere mortals and not God;
    their horses are flesh and not spirit. (Is 30:1-3; 31:3;
        see Jer 2:36-37)

Given, then, that the gods of the nations were a disappointing failure even to the nations who worshiped them, and given that Yahweh alone was the living God who could be trusted not to fail, it was doubly tragic that Israel should even *think* of exchanging the one for the other. There is something grossly unnatural about it, as Jeremiah observes in shocked disbelief. The pagan nations stay obstinately loyal to the gods they have, even though they do not exist, while Israel swaps the only living God it knows for such nonentities!

> "Has a nation ever changed its gods?
>> (Yet they are not gods at all.)
> But my people have exchanged their glorious God
>> for worthless idols.
> Be appalled at this, you heavens,
>> and shudder with great horror,"
>>> declares the LORD.
> "My people have committed two sins:
> They have forsaken me,
>> the spring of living water,
> and have dug their own cisterns,
>> broken cisterns that cannot hold water." (Jer 2:11-13)

How could anyone abandon a guaranteed source of life for a guaranteed source of disappointment? Yet that is what Israel has done, in forsaking its spring of living water for a leaking cistern. "Broken cisterns that can hold no water" are a powerful image of disappointment, futility, and wasted effort.

The Lord himself then chides Israel for the ungrateful futility of its folly. Drawing from the ancient tradition of Deuteronomy 32:37-38, Jeremiah depicts just how perverse Israel has become, in first turning away from Yahweh to worship despicable gods and then brazenly turning around and expecting Yahweh to save it when the multiple gods of its own manufacture utterly fail to deliver.

> They say to wood, "You are my father,"
>> and to stone, "You gave me birth."[6]

They have turned their backs to me
  and not their faces;
yet when they are in trouble, they say,
  "Come and save us!"
Where then are *the gods you made for yourselves?*
  Let them come if they can save you
  when you are in trouble!
For you, Judah, have as many gods
  as you have towns. (Jer 2:27-28 emphasis added)

Kings, armies, horses, treaties, riches, natural resources—all these things are *not* really gods and are unable to bear the weight of trust we put in them. However, what makes them into gods is that we insist on believing the spurious promises they make (or that we implicitly attribute to them). We keep on paying the enormous sacrifices they demand for our loyalty. We keep on hoping against hope that they will not let us down. But of course, they always do in the end. Idolatry is wasted effort and dashed hopes.

The worship of false gods is the fellowship of futility, the grand delusion whose only destiny is disappointment.

So when an editorial in a British national newspaper once concluded its sad analysis of a society in which two children could callously murder a toddler with the words "All our gods have failed," it doubtless intended the words only as a figure of speech.[7] Sadly, such a metaphorical cry of despair also precisely captures the spiritual truth. Those things we thought could deliver us from evil, and in which we invested great amounts of intellectual, financial, and emotional capital in the hope that they would deliver us, have instead spectacularly disappointed us.

When will we ever learn?

CHAPTER FOUR

MISSION AND THE GODS

HAVING IDENTIFIED HOW the Bible portrays some of the ways
in which and the reasons why human beings manufacture gods
and idols, and the damage they do to ourselves and our relationship with
the living God, how should we go about the task of dealing with them
in the many different social, cultural, evangelistic, and pastoral contexts
in which we are called to minister? Once again, the Bible provides some
vitally important insights for our missional engagement.

Remembering that the battle is the Lord's

The Bible clearly portrays the struggle with idolatry as a *battle* between
Yahweh, the living God, and all those forces that oppose him. Johannes
Verkuyl explains:

> The whole Old Testament (and the New Testament as well) is filled
> with descriptions of how Yahweh-Adonai, the covenant God of
> Israel, is waging war against those forces which try to thwart and
> subvert his plans for his creation. He battles against those false gods
> which human beings have fashioned from the created world, idolised,
> and used for their own purpose. Think, for example, of the Baals and
> the Ashteroth, whose worshippers elevated nature, the tribe, the
> state, and the nation to a divine status. God fights against magic and
> astrology which, according to Deuteronomy, bend the line between
> God and his creation. He contends against every form of social in-
> justice and pulls off every cloak under which it seeks to hide.[1]

He mentions the gods of the Canaanite cults, but we could equally think of the great battle with the unnamed gods of Egypt in the exodus narrative (see Ex 12:12) that preceded Israel's life in Canaan, or of the sustained rhetorical polemic against the gods of Babylon in the context of Israel's exile in the book of Isaiah.[2]

Now that we have surveyed the dismal devastation that idolatry wreaks in human life, we can see this conflict between God and the gods in a fresh light. I will make three points of missional relevance.

The missional love of God repels idolatry. On the one hand it is true, as we have seen, that God battles with idolatry because it diminishes the glory that is rightfully God's own. God's jealousy for God's own self is a powerful dynamic throughout Scripture. But on the other hand, God's battle against the gods of human hands (and all they represent) can be seen as a function of his *loving benevolence toward us* and indeed toward his whole creation. Divine jealousy is in fact an essential function of divine love. It is precisely because God wills our good that he hates the self-inflicted harm that our idolatry generates. God's conflict with the gods is ultimately for our own good, as well as for God's glory.

This further highlights why idolatry is such a primary sin in the Bible—identified as such by the primacy of the first two commandments of the Decalogue. It is not merely that idolatry steals God's glory but also that it thwarts God's love—the love that seeks the highest good of all God's creation. Idolatry therefore contradicts the very essence, the God-ness, of God, for God is love.

It is important to take note of a strongly missional hermeneutic in our discussion. We are not approaching this matter from the perspective of an attempted reconstruction of the evolution of Israel's religion, nor merely from the perspective of the religious psychology of those who worshiped other gods. We remind ourselves constantly that the primary driving force of the biblical grand narrative is the priority of God's own mission. Israel's religion at the empirical level of popular practice seems to have ebbed and flowed in terms of its commitment to the monotheistic dynamic within it, and more often than not it succumbed to ambient polytheism. But *the canon as a whole* bears witness to the persistent determination of the living God, in transcendent uniqueness and universality, to defeat and destroy all that seduces human beings away from the love they receive from God and the love they should give to God.

God's battle with the gods, then, is an essential part of God's mission. And God's mission is the blessing of the nations. So the blessing of the nations must ultimately include ridding them of gods that masquerade as protectors and saviors but are actually devouring, destroying, disappointing deceptions. The battle to rid the nations of their false gods is a battle of divine love.

The battle and the victory belong to God. Second, by putting our emphasis on the mission of God, not on human mission or missions, we preserve the right biblical perspective on this matter. For we need to be clear that in the Bible *the conflict with the gods is a conflict waged by God for us, not a conflict waged by us for God.* To be sure, the people of God are involved in spiritual warfare, as countless texts in both Testaments testify. However, it is assuredly *not* the case that God is waiting anxiously for the day when we finally win the battle for him and the heavens can applaud our great victory. Such blasphemous nonsense, however, is not far removed from the rhetoric and practice of some forms of alleged mission that place great store on all kinds of methods and techniques of warfare by which we are urged to identify and defeat our spiritual enemies. No, the overwhelming emphasis of the Bible is that *we* are the ones who wait in hope for the day when *God* defeats all the enemies of God and his people, and then we will celebrate *God's* victory along with angels, archangels, and all the company of heaven. Indeed, in the company of heaven we already celebrate the victory of the cross and resurrection of Christ, the Easter victory that anticipates the final destruction of all God's enemies.

It is God who fights for us, not we who fight for him. We are called to witness, to struggle, to resist, to suffer. But the battle is the Lord's, as is the final victory.

Our battle is fought with love, not triumphalism. Third, insofar as our mission undoubtedly also includes the dimension of spiritual warfare, we need to recognize that our primary aim is not to "win" but to serve. That is to say: the idols, gods, demons, and spiritual powers, against which we declare war in the name of the gospel of Christ and his cross, are things that oppress and ravage human existence. False gods destroy and devour lives, health, and resources; they distort and diminish our humanity; they preside over injustice, greed, perversion, cruelty, lust, and violence. It is possibly the most satanic dimension of their deceptive power that, in spite of all this, they still persuade people that they are the beneficent protectors of their worshipers' identity, dignity, and prosperity, and must therefore be defended at all costs. Only the gospel can unmask these claims. Only the gospel exposes the cancer of idolatry. Only the gospel is good for people.

Our missional motivation, therefore, needs to be carefully examined. Spiritual warfare is not a matter of triumphalism, pervaded by a horrid spirit of gloating superiority, in which we become obsessed with winning a victory. Rather, it is a matter of deep compassion for those oppressed by the forces of evil and idolatry—with all their attendant social, economic, political, spiritual, and personal effects. We battle with idolatry because, like the God whose mission we thereby share, we know that in doing so we seek the best interests of those we are called to serve in his name. We combat idolatry not only to glorify God but also to bless humanity. Spiritual warfare, like all forms of biblical mission, is to be motivated by and exercised with profound love, humility, and compassion—as modeled in Jesus himself.

Confronting idolatry in varied contexts

Combating idolatry can take many forms. The Bible itself prepares us to recognize that different approaches may be relevant in different contexts. Wisdom in mission calls us to be discerning and to recognize that what may be appropriate in one situation may not be so helpful in another. Within the ministry of the apostle Paul, for example, we may observe the different approach adopted when, for example, he tackles idolatry in the context of dense theological argument of a letter written to believers versus when he is confronting it in evangelistic engagement with the worshipers of other gods, and again versus when he is wrestling pastorally with questions raised within the church about surrounding idolatry. To these we may add the prophetic conflict with idolatry, which exposes its futility but does so primarily for the ears of the people of God.

Defining idolatry in theological argument. Writing to Christians, and speaking of idolatry objectively as a phenomenon, Paul pulls no punches. In his sharp analysis of human rebellion against God in Romans 1:18-32, he sets idolatry firmly within the realm of that which incurs the wrath of God. It is the result of deliberate suppression of the truth about God that is known and available to all humans. It involves the inversion of the creation order, exchanging the worship of the living God for the worship of images of creation. It claims wisdom but is rank folly. It issues in a catalogue of vice and viciousness, polluting every aspect of human life— sexual, social, familial, and personal. Idolatry is alienating, darkening, degrading, divisive, and deadly. We must not separate any part of this analysis from the whole. Paul's attack on idolatry is theological, intellectual, spiritual, ethical, and social. It is a powerful piece of theological argument, preparatory to his exposition of the fullness of the gospel.

Mission requires that we engage in such discourse when appropriate, for we have no liberty to dilute the lurid colors of Paul's exposure of idolatry here. This is the truth of the matter, the distillation of so many other biblical texts on the subject. The good news of the gospel has to be seen (as it very soon is in Romans) against the horrendously bad news of what human addiction to idolatry actually is. However, to repeat: the *context* here is tight theological argument, the prelude to Paul's full exposition of the gospel as "the power of God that brings salvation to everyone who believes: first for the Jew, then for the Gentile" (Rom 1:16). These words are written by Paul *to Christians,* as words of teaching and warning for Christians. We need to face up to the full truth and viciousness of what idolatry is and what it does.

Challenging idolatry in evangelistic engagement. The book of Acts gives us three glimpses of Paul in direct contact with pagan worshipers of the gods of the Greek culture:

- in Lystra (Acts 14:8-20)
- in Athens (Acts 17:16-34)
- in Ephesus (Acts 19:23-41)

The circumstances were very different in each location, but there are some interesting common features.

In Lystra, the healing of a cripple led to Barnabas and Paul being hailed as the Greek gods Zeus and Hermes in human form, and to a sacrifice being prepared in their honor. Paul countered with strong protestations of their own mere humanity and followed this with an appeal that the crowd should turn from "these worthless things" to the one living God, Creator of heaven and earth, who had been giving them all the good things of life.

In Athens, discussions with some philosophers about Jesus and the resurrection led to a summons before the city authorities, the Areopagus, to submit his teaching to their inspection. This hearing was probably not merely a matter of polite curiosity but a public inquiry. "Introducing new gods into Athens" (as they thought Paul was trying to do) was not a necessarily a problem religiously, but it had to be controlled by the civic authorities, to ensure that (1) claimed deities actually had some track record to their name and (2) the sponsor could afford to set up a temple, provide the sacrifices, pay the priests, and so on.[3] Paul's speech stands this civic protocol on its head. The God he represented was not subject to human accreditation by the Athenian authorities but rather sat in judgment on them. Far from needing the services of human attendants for housing and feeding, it was this God who provided these things and much more for the whole human race.

In Ephesus, two years of systematic public lecturing (Acts 19:9-10), accompanied by remarkable healing miracles (Acts 19:11-12), led to growth in truly converted believers (Acts 19:17-20). So many people were turning to the living God through faith in Christ that the bottom began to drop out of the market for the idol industry in the city (Acts 19:23-27). We have no direct record of Paul's teaching, but Luke summarizes it in the mouth of Demetrius: "He [Paul] says that gods made by human hands are no gods at all" (Acts 19:26).

The monotheistic message of the gospel thus challenged popular superstition in Lystra, intellectual and civic pride in Athens, and economic interests in Ephesus. The thrust of Paul's evangelistic tactics in such circumstances—for example, when engaging directly with idol-worshiping pagans, as distinct from offering theological teaching to established believers—is forthright and uncompromising but markedly softer and more polite than the language we observe in Romans 1.

In the two recorded speeches (in Lystra and Athens), Paul emphasizes God as the one living Creator of heaven and earth (Acts 14:15; 17:24). In both he stresses the providence of God in giving humans all the necessities of life, even life and breath itself (Acts 14:17; 17:25). In Lystra he offers this as evidence of the kindness of God, bringing joy even to pagans; in Athens he offers it as proof that God longs for people to seek him, though he is in fact not far from any of us (supporting this from pagan poetry; Acts 17:27-28). In both places, he allows that God has been patient and tolerant of pagan ignorance in the past (Acts 14:16; 17:30). But in both he also calls for a decisive turning away from the worship of "worthless things" (Acts 14:15), which are hopelessly inadequate for the divine being (Acts 17:29). This is consistent with his own testimony regarding the burden of his preaching in Thessalonica. He recalls how pagans there had "turned to God from idols to serve the living and true God" (1 Thess 1:9). In Athens, he goes on to speak of judgment and to link it to the resurrection of Christ (Acts 17:31).

What we learn from the lips of the pagans themselves in Ephesus is that Paul argued that manmade gods are not gods at all (Acts 19:26—a thoroughly Old Testament perspective, as we have seen). But we also learn, most interestingly, that Paul had *not* engaged in specific defamation of Artemis/Diana, the patron goddess of Ephesus. This is not even a claim Paul makes for himself but is stated in his defense by the city clerk to pacify the riot fomented against Paul and his friends. *"They have neither robbed temples nor blasphemed our goddess"* (Acts 19:37 italics added). Clearly Paul's evangelism was uncompromisingly effective but not calculatingly offensive. Paul could speak the truth with grace and respect.

He did not have to disparage and demean his listeners in order to display and commend the gospel. We could learn from him.

Comparing Paul's *theological* argument to Christians in Romans 1 with his *evangelistic* preaching to pagans recorded in Acts, there is a marked difference of tone, even though there is certainly no clash of fundamental conviction. It is the same theology but in different tones.

- Romans, written to Christians, highlights the wrath of God. Acts, in recording speeches made to pagans, highlights God's kindness, providence, and patience. Both, however, do explicitly insist on God's judgment.
- Romans portrays idolatry as fundamentally rebellion and suppression of the truth. Acts portrays it as ignorance.
- Romans portrays the wickedness that idolatry spawns. Acts portrays idolatry as "worthless."
- Romans points out how perverted the idolater's thinking has to be. Acts points out how absurd it is when you stop and think about it.
- Paul could excoriate idolatry as "a lie" before Christian readers but did not blaspheme Artemis before her pagan worshipers.

So there is a difference in tone and tactic in Paul's confrontation with idolatry depending on the context of his argument. However, we should be clear that in both cases, he is building all he has to say on very solid scriptural foundations, for every one of the points mentioned above, even though they have differing and balancing emphases, can be related to the Old Testament's rhetoric against idolatry, as we have seen. It is particularly noteworthy that, although Paul nowhere quotes Old Testament texts in his evangelistic preaching among Gentiles (as he so profusely does when speaking among Jews in synagogues), the content of his message is thoroughly grounded in, and plainly proclaims, the monotheistic creational faith of Israel.

Explaining idolatry for pastoral guidance. Those who came to faith in Christ out of a background of Greco-Roman polytheism embraced the biblical monotheistic worldview. But they still lived surrounded by all the idolatrous phenomena of the culture within which they were now called to live out their Christian identity. This posed daily dilemmas for them. The thoroughness of Paul's mission practice is that he was not content merely with evangelism and church planting but was concerned to build mature communities of believers who could think biblically through the ethical issues they faced in the ambient religious culture. His pastoral and ethical guidance to his churches was thus as much a part of his missional task as his evangelistic zeal, and just as theologically grounded too.

First Corinthians 8–10 is the prime text on this matter. How are Christians to act in relation to meat that has been sacrificed to idols? The nub of the issue for the Corinthians is not primarily *theological* clarification: it seems the Corinthians know their theology, since Paul assumes it by way of reminder in 1 Corinthians 8:4-6. Nor is it primarily *evangelistic*: the Corinthians have already come to faith in Jesus Christ (1 Cor 1:1-9). But it is certainly *pastoral and ethical,* since there are divisions within the church on the matter, and some members are being hurt and offended, while others are being arrogant and reckless.

We have already discussed the passage in some depth in chapter one, around the question, Are gods and idols something or nothing? so we need not go over that ground again. However, it is worth recalling that there were two aspects to the problem, and Paul gives a distinct answer to each. Both have a bearing on how Christians deal with the practical problems of ambient idolatry.

On the one hand, there is *the ordinary meat market.* Animals were slaughtered in sacrificial rituals to various gods, and then the meat would end up on the butcher's slab in the market. Could Christians buy such meat in the market and serve it up without endorsing the prior idolatry involved in its production? Paul's answer is, in general terms, "Yes, you may. The gods and idols have no real existence; meat as food is a good gift of God the Creator and can be enjoyed in thankfulness to him." The only exception to this freedom is if it causes offense to someone else at the table—in which case you should refrain out of respect for that other person's more tender conscience. The rule of love takes precedence over the freedom one legitimately has. Apart from that restriction, "eat anything sold in the meat market" is Paul's down-to-earth advice (1 Cor 10:25).

But on the other hand, there are the meals that were hosted actually within the precincts of *the temples of the gods*, often as civic functions or as social events put on by wealthier citizens. These were opportunities for securing patronage, making advantageous deals, and fitting in with the social expectations of the Corinthian elite. Since these involved actual participation in the sacrifices in the temples of the gods (as distinct from simply going to the butcher's stall and buying meat that was a byproduct of the sacrifice), Paul would not endorse Christians attending such events.

Now, Paul knew full well the negative social consequences for Christians of such self-exclusion from gatherings at the temples. Christians who declined invitations to such regular sacrifice feasts at the temples would not merely be seen to be negligent or offensive to the city's gods; they would also miss out on opportunities for social networking and very likely endanger their relationship with patrons and employers. But Paul was adamant. Stay away.

First of all, attendance at such feasts in the temples, even done with full theological knowledge of their emptiness, poses a far greater threat to the conscience of the weaker brother or sister who sees you doing it, and so if you insist on your mature freedoms you could be sinning against Christ, who died for them (1 Cor 8:10-13). But second, even though the idols and sacrifices are nothing in any divine sense, they can certainly be doorways to the demonic. Christians cannot mix participation in the body and blood of Christ with participation in the feasts of demons (1 Cor 10:14-22). For that reason, Paul's advice on *this* part of the question is simple: "flee from idolatry" (1 Cor 10:14)—that is, do not allow any suspicion that you are participating in it, even if you have your internal theological defenses up. Stay away.

The subtlety and sensitivity with which Paul constructs the pastoral and ethical application of his theology (i.e., the missiological implications of radical monotheism in the context of a powerful cultural polytheism) is very illuminating. It surely has much to offer to Christians in many different religious and cultural contexts, caught in the pressure between theological conviction and social conventions.

In contexts where other named gods are explicitly worshiped, Christians may have to distinguish between the byproducts of rituals associated with those gods and actual participation in the worship of them. Some Christians in India, for example, feel free to accept *prasad*—the gifts of sweets or fruits from Hindu friends or work colleagues who have celebrated a birthday or other event by offering something first to the gods in their home or place of work. But they are not willing to join in actual rituals, or to participate in multifaith worship, or anything that explicitly affirms the reality of other gods. Other Indian Christians exclude both for fear of misleading "the weaker brother."

In the West, gods and idols take more subtle forms, but similar issues may arise. Gambling, for example, could certainly be conceived as a form of idolatry to the god of Mammon, with all the tendency to addiction that most idolatries feed. For that reason most Christians see it as an ethical issue and refuse to engage in it or intentionally to set out to profit from it, either by participating in gambling (e.g., state lotteries) or by requesting money from the organizers of such lotteries. We do not do gambling, as a participant or profitee. On the other hand, if someone who wins the lottery chooses, unasked, to give some of the money to the church or a Christian charity, there are those who would argue that such money can be accepted without raising questions of conscience, since all wealth belongs to the Lord in the first place. You are not participating in the evil of gambling by accepting such a gift, even though it was the product of gambling, any more than a Corinthian was participating in idolatry by buying meat at the butcher's shop, even though it was produced in an idolatrous ritual. Other Christians would refuse such a gift because of its source to avoid being complicit in the original act, which they see as sinful. Disagreement on this among Western Christians is as likely as that over *prasad* among Indian Christians.

Doubtless many other examples of the outworking of Paul's pastoral and ethical guidelines could be discussed. My point is that his handling of the matter in a pastoral context among new Christian believers has a different feel from either his evangelistic engagement with nonbelievers or his theological invective in a strongly didactic context for mature Christians. Perhaps we have something to learn from Paul in the way we confront idolatry in our own multiple contexts. Of course, before we even get around to such pastoral and ethical discussion, we have to actually *recognize and discern* the presence of idolatry and false gods in our own midst—which many Christians in the West at least seem unable or reluctant to do. That calls for the same courage as the prophets of Israel showed. And so to our final response:

Exposing idolatry with prophetic warning. The pastoral approach that we have just been considering involves helping God's people to cope with the dilemmas of living in a culture in which idolatry is endemic. The prophetic approach, however, involves identifying, exposing, and denouncing the idolatry itself. But it is noteworthy that where this happens in the Bible it is normally *for the ears of God's people.* That is where idolatry is at its most vile and damaging.

As we have seen, in evangelistic contexts in the New Testament, there is unambiguous repudiation of the polytheistic worldview, but we do not find public denunciation of specific gods or offensive mockery of their worshipers. In the Old Testament, in the few places where an Israelite addresses pagan nations, the condemnation is typically targeted at their moral and social wickedness, not at their worship of the wrong gods (even though the two are connected, as we have seen). Examples of this might include Amos's catalogue of the sins of the nations surrounding Israel (Amos 1:1–2:3—noticeably, Amos only specifies worship of false gods when he gets around to Judah in Amos 2:4) and Jonah's condemnation of Nineveh, which is explicitly aimed at "its wickedness" and "their violence," not their gods (Jonah 1:2; 3:8). Elijah's mockery of the prophets of Baal should be seen not as the mockery of ignorant pagans, for many of those prophets were actually apostates from Yahwism. Their main offense was in leading the people into their own idolatrous confusion.

However, no rhetorical device is redundant when prophetic voices address their denunciation of idolatry *to the people of God themselves*. We need only recall the penetrating polemic of Isaiah 40–48, or the similar arguments of Jeremiah 10, or the warnings of Deuteronomy 4. What is the reason for this heavy imbalance? Why so little condemnation of their false gods when addressing the pagan nations, and such relentless polemic against other gods when addressing Israel?

Of course it was true that idolatry was to be avoided for fear of incurring the jealous wrath of the living God (Paul was no stranger to that argument either; see 1 Cor 10:22). But prophets also exposed the futility of idolatry in order *to release God's people from undue fear of the gods of nations* that seemed more powerful. This is obvious in Isaiah 40–48. It is also Jeremiah's motivation:

> Do not learn the ways of the nations
>> or be terrified by signs in the heavens,
>> though the nations are terrified by them. . . .
> Like a scarecrow in a cucumber field,
>> their idols cannot speak;
> they must be carried
>> because they cannot walk.
> Do not fear them;
>> they can do no harm
>> nor can they do any good. (Jer 10:2, 5)

Prophets also denounce the gods of the nations because they know that Israel will ultimately only be disappointed and humiliated if it goes after them. Warning God's people against idolatry is for their own protection. The cost is too high—as Israel in exile discovered, through the retrospective explanations of Ezekiel.

It would not be out of place to include Romans 1:18-32 in this company of the prophets, for Paul's searing exposure of the perverse roots and bitter fruit of idolatry stands in the same prophetic tradition. Like the prophets of old, Paul summons the redeemed people of God to see idolatry *from God's point of view* and recognize the appalling truth about what they have been redeemed from.

Ephesus provides another interesting case study. As we saw from Acts, Paul preached the gospel in Ephesus, and many people turned from idolatry and sorcery to the living God. In the course of that church-planting program, Paul did not indulge in public defamation of Artemis (according to the secular authorities). Yet in writing later to those new believers in Ephesus who had chosen to turn away from their worship of Artemis and trust in Christ, Paul did not hesitate to remind them of their parlous spiritual state *before* they came to faith in Christ. They had been alienated from Israel, from Israel's Messiah, from Israel's covenant hope, and from Israel's God. In fact, in an ironic turn of phrase, Paul says that these Ephesians, with all their many gods, had in fact been *atheoi*—"without God"—inasmuch as they had no knowledge of or relationship with the true and living God (Eph 2:12). Being without God (in spite of their many gods, not least Artemis), they had been "without hope."

Later again Paul reminds the Ephesians of the kind of life they had been rescued from—a life characterized by precisely those things Paul elsewhere so closely links with idolatry in Romans 1 (futility, darkness, hardness, sensual indulgence, etc.; Eph 4:17-19). Part of Paul's purpose in writing thus is to remind believers of the moral and spiritual darkness of idolatry, to warn them against ever going back to it, and to encourage them to live the distinctive holy life of the redeemed. It seems clear that Paul attacked idolatry much more fiercely in discipling those who had been delivered from it than he did in his public evangelistic ministry among those still involved in it. This mirrors the same imbalance that we observed in the Old Testament prophets. *It is God's people who need the most warning against the dangers of idolatry* and to be made aware of what they have been delivered from and should not go back to.

In what way is this prophetic warning to the people of God against idolatry in both Old and New Testaments missiologically significant?

The answer lies in appreciating the mission of God in and through God's people. God's goal of blessing the nations requires not only that the nations eventually come to abandon their gods and bring their worship before the living God alone (as envisaged, for example, in Ps 96 and many prophetic visions). God's mission also requires that God's own people in the meantime should preserve the purity and exclusiveness of their worship of the living God, and resist the adulterating syncretisms that surround them. An obedient and covenantally loyal Israel would be seen by the nations, and the result would be praise and glory to Yahweh the living God (Deut 4:6-8; 28:9-10). A disobedient and idolatrous Israel would bring disgrace on Yahweh and drag his name through the gutters of profanity among the nations (Deut 29:24-28; Ezek 36:16-21). In other words, more is at stake in keeping God's people away from idols than their own spiritual health. God's own mission for the sake of the nations is also on the line.

Jeremiah, with his customary graphic imagery, captures both sides of this perception of the mission of Israel in a single piece of prophetic acted symbolism (Jer 13:1-11). As a beautiful piece of clothing brings honor and praise to the one who wears it, so God had bound Israel to himself "to be my people for my renown and praise and honor" (Jer 13:11).[4] This triplet of words is the same as that which God had promised Israel would have among the nations (Deut 26:19). Whatever renown may accrue to God's people through their loyalty and obedience to him, is ultimately for the honor and glory of God himself. That is the missiological dynamic.

But the effect of Israel's idolatry (specified in Jer 13:10) is to make it like a beautiful piece of cloth that has been buried in wet soil for a long time—"ruined and completely useless" (Jer 13:7, 10). God cannot "wear" people who are sodden and soiled with the rotting rags of idolatry. How can God draw the nations away from the worship of false gods, if the people he has chosen to be a blessing to the nations are themselves riddled with those gods? The scorching severity of the warnings against idolatry, then, are not just for the benefit of God's own people but ultimately, through them, for the benefit of the nations. That is their missional relevance. God's people must keep themselves from false gods, not just for their own sake but for the sake of their mission, or rather, of God's mission among the nations.

Conclusion

Let us summarize what we have seen in these chapters of part one concerning the missiological dimension of the Bible's polemic against idolatry.

- We have seen the paradox that although gods and idols are something in the world, they are nothing in comparison to the living God.
- We have seen that while gods and idols may be implements of or gateways to the world of the demonic, the overwhelming verdict of Scripture is that they are the work of human hands, constructs of our own fallen and rebellious imagination.
- We have also seen that the primal problem with idolatry is that it blurs the distinction between the Creator God and the creation. This both damages creation (including ourselves) and diminishes the glory of the Creator.
- Since God's mission is to restore the whole of creation to its full original purpose of bringing glory to God himself, and thereby to enable all creation to enjoy the fullness of blessing that God desires for it, God battles against all forms of idolatry and calls us to join him in that conflict.
- A biblically informed, missional approach to idolatry, however, seeks to understand the great variety of ways in which human beings make gods for themselves, the variety of forms those gods take, and the variety of motivations behind our worship of them.
- Then also, we need to understand the whole breadth of the Bible's exposure of the deleterious effects of idolatry, in order to appreciate its seriousness and the reason for the Bible's passionate rhetoric about it.

- Finally, in confronting idolatry, we need to be discerning about what responses are appropriate in different contexts, learning from the apostles and prophets as we do so.

All of these tasks need to be carried on not only in the light of the wide range of biblical texts such as those we have touched on in these chapters but also in relation to specific cultural and religious contexts and their particular manifestations of the human addiction to idolatry. The prophets and apostles set us the clear example of both claiming universality and transcendence for Yahweh and Christ, and at the same time engaging with cutting relevance in the particular and local contexts into which they were sent. Our mission demands no less. To that latter task we turn in part two.

Part two

POLITICAL IDOLATRY THEN AND NOW

THE TITLE GIVEN TO ME for the lecture that lies behind part two was "Following Jesus in an Age of Political Turbulence." In preparing for it, the hardest part was combining the two halves of the title itself.

If I had been asked to speak just on following Jesus, I could have given a straightforward account of discipleship and a few challenging exhortations from some well-known Bible texts. A biblical lecture on discipleship? No problem.

If I had been asked just to comment on the momentous political changes of the previous year, I would probably have declined. I am usually willing to share my opinions in private conversation, but it is not at all my habit to expatiate on politics in a public lecture setting—especially when I am a guest in another country. Just stick to the Bible.

But putting the two phrases together? This forcibly reminded me that, of course, the Bible itself does this. You cannot really just stick to the Bible and be faithful to the Bible as a whole *without* connecting it to the political world, since the context of so many of the biblical texts is precisely that—the public world of politics, economics, government, law, and so on. So the invitation challenged me, forced me, to think in *biblical* categories about what appears to be happening in the world today—especially in the Western world in general, and the United Kingdom and United States in particular.

Surely that *ought* to be the task of those of us who are (whether deservedly or not) viewed as biblical experts. It is our responsibility not just to expound the Bible in general terms but to discern how it still speaks into the contemporary world. That intuition led John Stott to launch the highly popular series of expositions on Bible books known as The Bible Speaks Today. It also led him to his well-known tactic of double listening—that is, he would say, we must listen to the *Word* (that is, study and understand, believe and obey the Bible), *and* we must listen to the *world* (that is, understand our own culture, its good and bad features, its questions and critique).

Bringing the Bible to bear on contemporary politics is usually very uncomfortable, for it exposes so much that we would prefer should stay hidden and even more that we may not have seen at all—such as the idols that dominate so much of our public and political life. Yet the whole idea of gods and idols, though it is such a prominent theme in the Bible (especially in the arena of public and national life), seems damagingly neglected in contemporary Christian political discourse and analysis.

That observation lies behind my choice of title for the book—*Here Are Your Gods*—and its relevance to this second part.

On both occasions when these words are exclaimed in the Old Testament, there is an ironic ambiguity. The people of Israel say this when they see the golden calf that Aaron fashions at the start of the great apostasy while Moses is on Mount Sinai with God (Ex 32:4). Jeroboam says this after he fashions two golden calves at either end of his kingdom as a political act of consolidating and sanctifying his state power (1 Kings 11:28).

On both occasions the words are followed by "who brought you up out of Egypt." So there is a desire somehow to identify these idols with Yahweh, their uniquely powerful, saving God. Yet, as carved images, they are what they are—idols! They stand there in blatant breach of the first and second of the Ten Commandments. This is the essence of syncretism. The Israelites want to claim that they are still loyally worshiping Yahweh, the living God, and yet they are creating and submitting to idols of their own manufacture. They cannot entirely let go of the God of their history, yet they rebelliously make gods for themselves—and in the second instance for blatantly political ends. National idolatry started early. It was the original sin of Jeroboam, as we saw in chapter two.

In the tattered remnants of Christendom that still survive in the Western world, particularly in the United States and United Kingdom, the monosyllable *God* still tends to mean, in the popular mind or imagination, God as presumed within the Christian heritage of Western civilization—however much rejected, renounced, secularized, and threatened that heritage certainly is. So when God turns up at all in public speech ("In God we trust," "God bless America," "God save the Queen," "We don't do God"), this is the imagined God—omnipresent, perhaps, but omni-impotent and omni-irrelevant.[1] The "real" gods—the ones laughing in obfuscating gloom as they pull the levers of political, economic, and cultural power—are the false gods and idols that humans have bowed down to for millennia and still do in all their shiny modern seductiveness. As Christians we desperately need to name them and expose them. "Here are your gods!"

But at the same time, returning to the task in hand, this effort of bringing the Word to bear on the world is also ultimately reassuring. For it reminds us that we should be living in and for the story we are actually part of (the Bible's great redemptive story, culminating in the ultimate rectification of the final judgment and the glory of the new creation), not just the story that is being spun around us. That biblical story is filled with hope, for it is the story of the sovereign mission and kingdom of God that will ultimately triumph over all human empires. How then should we live, as followers of Jesus—Messiah, Savior, Lord, and King?

That is the task to which we turn in part two.

CHAPTER FIVE

THE RISE AND FALL OF NATIONS IN BIBLICAL PERSPECTIVE

THE LONG STORY OF SUCCESSIVE EMPIRES that the Old Testament tells indicates a pattern that repeats throughout history, under the sovereign governance of the Lord God of Israel. The Torah, prophets, and the psalms and Wisdom writings all affirm that God rules over all nations, and that they rise and fall according to the criteria he has established for human life on earth.[1]

God made this clear to the pharaoh, the self-deified ruler of the Egyptian empire. "For by now I could have stretched out my hand and struck you and your people with a plague that would have wiped you off the earth. But I have raised you up for this very purpose, that I might show you my power and that my name might be proclaimed in all the earth" (Ex 9:15-16).

God informs the Israelites that, just as he is giving them the land of Canaan, so he has given other lands to other nations whom he, Yahweh, has been moving around on the chessboard of history for centuries. Deuteronomy 2:1-23 affirms, almost as incidental footnotes, the sovereignty of Yahweh over all nations. It was Yahweh, not the gods of the Moabites, Ammonites, Rephaites, Avvites, and Zamzumites (whoever they were), who had driven one nation out before another and settled people in different lands. Giving Israel a land to live in was nothing new for God and, in and of itself, nothing unique in history (as Amos later insists; see Amos 9:7).

Isaiah portrays the God of Israel raising up and bringing down the kings of the earth—an astonishing claim in view of the intended target— the power of Babylon.

> He brings princes to naught
>> and reduces the rulers of this world to nothing.
> No sooner are they planted,
>> no sooner are they sown,
>> no sooner do they take root in the ground,
> than he blows on them and they wither,
>> and a whirlwind sweeps them away like chaff. (Is 40:23-24)

The psalmist and the wisdom writers likewise affirm that, while human authorities make their own plans and are accountable for those decisions and actions, God remains in ultimate control of historical outcomes. His word prevails in the end.

> The LORD foils the plans of the nations;
>> he thwarts the purposes of the peoples.
> But the plans of the LORD stand firm forever,
>> the purposes of his heart through all generations.
>> (Ps 33:10-11)

> In the LORD's hand the king's heart is a stream of water
>> that he channels toward all who please him. (Prov 21:1)

Even Nebuchadnezzar was brought to his knees to acknowledge "that the Most High is sovereign over all kingdoms on earth and gives them to anyone he wishes and sets over them the lowliest of people" (Dan 4:17). Daniel himself interpreted Nebuchadnezzar's dream statue in terms of the succession of empires that would rise and fall in the centuries to come (Dan 2).

This sustained and pervasive teaching of the Old Testament is not rejected or replaced in the New. On the contrary, the sovereign rule of

God over history and nations is placed in the hands of the risen Christ. He is, as John saw, the Lamb of God, crucified and risen, who stands at the center of the throne of God—the seat of universal governance (Rev 5:6). Jesus Christ is, as he claimed, "the ruler of the kings of the earth" (Rev 1:5). He is, in a passage reminiscent of Psalm 2, "KING OF KINGS AND LORD OF LORDS" (Rev 19:16), who will rule the nations with his iron scepter (Rev 19:15).

Moral principles and criteria

This sovereign governance of God over the rise and fall of nations, however, is not arbitrary. There are *moral principles* built into our world since creation, and they apply to all nations, even though they are explicitly revealed in the most articulated form in Israel. This is an important hermeneutical assumption that undergirds the whole second half of this book. God's revelation of his character and demands was made, of course, to Israel. But God's creation and election of Israel was *for the sake of the nations.* The standards that God required of Israel's socioeconomic and political life were intensified in the light of their experience of redemption and their covenant relationship with Yahweh, but they were consistent with the standards of righteousness and justice that the Creator and Judge of all people requires of all nations and governments.

Amos draws a noose around the neck of Judah and Israel by first condemning surrounding nations for their crimes against humanity, holding them accountable for their sins to the Lord God of Israel (Amos 1:1–2:8). If God judges *foreign* nations for their wickedness and crimes against humanity, how much more will God judge *Israel,* for whom he has done and said so much and who should know better? That is Amos's prime rhetorical point. But its effectiveness depends on its assumption: Yahweh is the God before whom *all* nations stand in judgment.

Jeremiah explicitly applies his imagery of the divine potter responding to the response of the "clay" in his hands not just to Judah but to any nation. The lesson of the potter and clay is not about mere personal submission to the will of God. Unfortunately, that is how it is often read and preached. Some sermons are more expositions of Adelaide A. Pollard's old hymn, which says, "Have thine own way, Lord, have thine own way / Thou art the Potter, I am the clay," than of the actual text and message of Jeremiah.[2] Jeremiah was not talking about personal piety but about God's moral sovereignty in international history.

> If at any time I announce that a nation or kingdom is to be uprooted, torn down and destroyed, and if that nation I warned repents of its evil, then I will relent and not inflict on it the disaster I had planned. And if at another time I announce that a nation or kingdom is to be built up and planted, and if it does evil in my sight and does not obey me, then I will reconsider the good I had intended to do for it. (Jer 18:7-10)

Unfortunately Jonah had not quite grasped the implications of the first half of that principle, but his book is a perfect case study of the principle in operation—to Jonah's great embarrassment and anger.

God may raise up nations and empires to accomplish his purposes, but when their arrogance, violence, and depravity reach an intolerable level, God acts in judgment and they collapse, or sink to levels of global insignificance, or even depart from the stage of history altogether. This is clearly stated by Isaiah in relation to the rising power of Assyria, which God used like a stick to punish Judah, and then in turn God acted in judgment on Assyria itself.

> "Woe to the Assyrian, the rod of my anger,
>   in whose hand is the club of my wrath!
> I send him against a godless nation,
>   I dispatch him against a people who anger me,
> to seize loot and snatch plunder,
>   and to trample them down like mud in the streets.
> But this is not what he intends,
>   this is not what he has in mind;
> his purpose is to destroy,
>   to put an end to many nations." . . .

When the Lord has finished all his work against Mount Zion and Jerusalem, he will say, "I will punish the king of Assyria for the willful pride of his heart and the haughty look in his eyes." (Is 10:5-7, 12)

Habakkuk addresses the same message to Babylon in turn, and Jeremiah reinforces it (Hab 2:4-20; Jer 50–51).

So then, in biblical times we see a sequence of empires, great and small, striding across the pages of history: Mesopotamia, Egypt, the Amorite nations in Canaan, Solomon's regional empire, the Assyrians, Babylonians, Persians, Greeks, Romans. . . . Some last a mere seventy years (Babylon), others seven hundred (Rome), but none lasts forever.

That is the key lesson. *All empires come to an end under the sovereign hand of God.* Perhaps one reason God superintended the production of the writings that form our canon of Scripture over so many centuries is that it gave the time and space to make this lesson very clear. The whole biblical narrative takes place in the midst of the rise and fall of empires, the ebb and flow of nations and governments and whole civilizations. God allowed it to go on and allows us, the readers of the Scriptures, to trace that sequence for hundreds and hundreds of years. We watch empires rise and fall, come and go, and God seems to be saying, "Don't you get the point yet?"

The collapse of these once-great nations and empires usually seems to include internal and external factors (which can be gleaned from both biblical records and other historical research into ancient empires). We can see

- *internal* corrosion (moral depravity, economic inequality and the resentment and rebellion it generated, excessive violence, political corruption, venality, nepotism, and greed) and
- *external* factors (changed economic conditions, e.g., caused by destruction of fertile land, or famine; the rise of rivals and enemies, or simply the arrival of younger and more aggressive cultures to which older declining ones fall prey).

So yes, there are many historical factors involved in why nations and empires in biblical times rose to dominance and then collapsed, sometimes spectacularly. Such factors are the stuff of historical research and interpretation. But the Bible goes further and deeper. Such collapse of empires and nations is also interpreted as the judgment of God, *mediated through those human circumstances and socioeconomic realities.* The historical process is not something separate from the governance of God. Rather, it embodies the outworking of the principles of God's governance. God is not trapped within the historical process, nor is God merely to be identified with it. He remains sovereign over it but is at work within and exercises his sovereignty through it.

All empires generate, thrive on, and depend on a degree of *arrogance,* usually combined with ethnocentric or racist pride and superiority. That kind of hubris—satanic in its origin but all too human in its manifestation—is quintessentially characteristic of our human fallenness. It is also abhorrent to God and ultimately self-destructive, for the principles of God's righteous governance of history work themselves out over time. When the sin of Adam and Eve that brought death to them is amplified and glorified at national and imperial levels, then it continues to bring death on the same scale. God's judgment is the outworking of our own arrogant and idolatrous choices, whether at personal or global levels. We reap what we sow. Eventually.

Falling and rising today?

What about our Western world, then? How do these biblical reflections and principles illumine where we find ourselves today?

It has long seemed to me that there are signs of something comparable to the collapse of those ancient biblical empires in these later decades of Western civilization in general, and in the social, economic, and political direction of the cultures of the United Kingdom and the United States in particular. I will mention some of those signs in a moment, but first let us sketch the historical perspective.

Approximately six hundred years ago, pre-Renaissance Western Europe was probably the world's poorest continent. The Black Death of the fourteenth century had wiped out an estimated 30 to 60 percent of the population. Far more advanced and wealthy empires were thriving in other parts of the world, including the Ashanti in West Africa, the Ottomans in the Middle East, the Ming Dynasty in China, the Aztecs in Central America, and Incas in the Andes.

Then, from the mid-fifteenth century on, Europeans embarked on a remarkable era of exploration and emigration that went on for some four centuries. They simply exported themselves gradually to all corners of the earth, settling (without permission or visas!) in the lands of other peoples, "discovering" continents and civilizations hitherto unknown to themselves, trading here, colonizing there, enslaving some, exterminating others. The inflow of astounding wealth and natural resources from all over the world slowly enriched European nations that were able to profit from it, and paved the way for the Industrial Revolution and the patterns and pathways of colonial rule and economic flows that followed. Europe and the countries predominantly built on European migration (North America and Australasia especially) rose to global hegemony as the heartlands of Western civilization, or simply "the West."

Five hundred years is a long time for any great civilization, history would tell us. Even the distinct imperial or colonial Western powers within that span lasted only a century or two—such as the Portuguese, Spanish, Dutch, French, Belgian, and even the British Empire itself. The heyday has passed. We seem to be a civilization in terminal decline, with shrinking birth rates and aging populations. If we apply the principles and scan the historical examples that the Bible sets before our eyes, it can be plausibly argued that the signs of decline and collapse, though they have many historical, social, and economic dimensions, may also be interpreted biblically as the slow outworking processes of God's moral judgment.

Internationally, the nineteenth century was dominated by the British Empire, and the twentieth century saw the United States rise to global leadership, and now it seems almost certain that the twenty-first century will eventually be China's. President Richard Nixon is said to have made this prediction a long time ago, and he seems likely to be correct. What will the rise of China to global prominence mean for the West by the end of this century, if Christ does not return before then? Only God knows.

But even as we contemplate that prospect, we should remember that God has been at work in China for more than a century, bringing somewhere around one hundred million people to the Christian faith.[3] Almost certainly there are now more people attending worship in Christian churches in China every Sunday than in the whole of Western Europe. The Chinese government is becoming ever more restrictive of Christian churches (as they are on Islam as well). Persecution and the expectation of suffering and imprisonment are now the normal lived experience of many believers there. But then, the same was true for Christians under the Roman Empire: steady numerical increase alongside periodic fierce persecution. But eventually Christianity transformed the Roman Empire from within in the fourth century, with the conversion of Constantine in 312 BC. God has enormous patience, and if a thousand years is as one day in his sight, what is a mere century?

What is God in his sovereign governance of history preparing for our world in such geopolitical and religious shifts and changes? What if China becomes a dominant world power and Chinese Christians eventually exercise a significant shift in the nation's cultural and political complexion and stance in the world? Not that we want anything like another Christendom. But just as the heartlands of Christianity globally have now already shifted from the West to the Global South (or the Majority World, as it is known), may we not also see a further shift to the Global East? As I said, only God knows, and I claim no prophetic mantle.

Now, it is very important to note what is *not* being suggested here. In comparing the declining West with the rise of China, I am not proposing that they are more righteous than we are, or anything so simplistic. The Old Testament warns Israel against that kind of binary assumption as to which nation is more righteous or more wicked than another (Deut 9:4-6). It was not to interpret its victory over the Canaanites as a claim to its own greater righteousness, any more than the later victory of the Assyrians or Babylonians over Israel would prove that they— those foreign nations—were somehow more righteous. God insists in Deuteronomy 9 that when God brings about the downfall of a nation or empire, it is on account of *its own wickedness.* When God brings one era of a dominant world power to an end and raises up another, it does not mean that the second, the newly emerging global player, is spotless and righteous in his sight. History, under God's governance, is not a Hollywood movie with simplistic, stereotyped bad guys and good guys.

Signs and symptoms

If we apply the biblical criteria provided by God's warnings to Israel and other nations, then Western civilization is in a spiral of decline that looks increasingly terminal. The signs and symptoms are many. Consider at least the following.

The legacy of historic and systemic violence. We live in societies that were historically founded on and continue to profit from genocide (of Native American and aboriginal peoples), centuries of African slavery on both sides of the Atlantic, rapacious colonialism, and lethally lucrative trade in weapons and proxy wars. In other words, our Western societies have enriched themselves through institutionalized and politically sanctioned breaking of at least three of the Ten Commandments, the ones forbidding murder, theft, and coveting, and have done so on a gigantic scale. There are centuries of blood on our hands, and the shedding of innocent blood is one of the most condemned political evils in the Old Testament for which the judgment of God eventually falls.

Apart from the last of those (the arms trade and profit from war), we may think that such evils lie in the past. But human slavery blights the lives of men, women, and children on a far greater scale today than in the days of William Wilberforce. Statistics from the Global Slavery

Index estimate that there were some 40.3 million victims of modern slavery on any given day in 2016.[4] It is reckoned that most of us in Western countries are the beneficiaries of some six or more slaves somewhere in the world, in the clothes we like to buy cheaply, the minerals in our cell phones, and even some of the food we enjoy.[5]

As regards genocide of native peoples and the arrogant predations and dictates of colonialism, the Old Testament shows that the effects of historic injustice and oppression are felt for centuries, and retribution for such evils may fall many generations later.[6] Proverbial chickens, unlike real ones, may outlive many human lifetimes before coming home to roost.

Increasing poverty and inequality. There is increasing neglect of the poor (not just in the Majority World but in our own Western nations), alongside unimaginable accumulation of wealth by the tiny few—the 0.1 percent. At the time of writing, reliable surveys estimate four million children are living in poverty in the United Kingdom (as defined by government metrics).[7] Absolute destitution and dependence on food banks has accelerated in the past decade. In the United States, some thirty-eight million people, or 11.8 percent of the population, live in poverty (again by government definition), and that includes 16.2 percent of all children.[8] Meanwhile we learn that a single minibus could hold the number of men whose combined wealth would balance that of the poorest half of the whole world's population.[9]

This growing inequality has become even worse since the global financial crisis of 2007–2009, which in its longer outcomes only served to increase the wealth of some while condemning whole swaths of the world's poor to paying the cost of the criminal folly of some Western banks. The grotesque imbalance of the superwealthy few alongside the struggles of impoverished many, in some of the richest nations on earth, must be as abominable in the eyes of God now as it was when the prophets raged against it in Old Testament Israel. It is well-researched that the more a society succumbs to greater inequality, the more it is likely to suffer from social instability and increasing violence.[10] Indeed, gross inequality is seen as a factor in the collapse of some of the great empires of history.[11]

The rise of extreme forms of populism and nationalism. Even though our nations have experienced the horrors of two world wars in the twentieth century, we seem to have learned nothing, as we witness the rise of political and populist attitudes, policies, and rhetoric reminiscent of the 1930s. White-supremacist movements and far-right parties, websites, and propaganda are enjoying a resurgence. The fracturing impact of identity politics and demagogues' skill at fostering a victim syndrome in the majority community while paradoxically asserting their own superiority and entitlement all play into a politics of fear and hatred of whatever "others" can be portrayed as the cause of social and economic malaise. Today's demagogues still use Pharaoh's playbook.

Meanwhile, there is hostility toward and denigration of institutions such as the United Nations and the European Union, which, while very far from perfect or free from the faults and flaws and endemic corruption that besets all human endeavors, have striven with some qualified success to keep the peace for half a century—at least in most of the endemically war-torn continent of Europe. Both the Brexit agenda and the "America First" mantra manifest a nationalist isolationism that seems to prefer competitive winners and losers to any kind of international, rules-based cooperation for collective benefit. This turns national interest into the law of the jungle. Every nation for itself, and let the strongest win. It is hard to see how this kind of hostile aggressive competitiveness can bless any civilization. Perhaps the idealism of a rules-based international order that emerged after the Second World War was the final effort of Western civilization to achieve some of its own higher values (largely derived in parasitic fashion from Christianity). So the collapse of those ideals and values in strident xenophobic nationalism seems to threaten a disintegration of the whole project.

Sexual confusion and family breakdown. There are some results of the sexual revolution and liberation of the 1960s that can be seen as positive and necessary: the greater emancipation of women and recognition of their equality in the workplace (even if a long way still from economic reality); the recognition of how hypocritical, unjust, and oppressive was the classic double-standard morality, in which women are blamed for infidelity or even rape and bear the stigma of illegitimate children, while men escape both punishment or even censure ("boys will be boys"); the decriminalization of homosexual intercourse between consenting adults.[12]

However, there have been disastrous long-term impacts as well. When sexual intimacy becomes no more than an appetite that can be satisfied as easily and as necessarily as hunger, then it migrates from the realm of deep and lifelong committed personal relationship into the realm of recreational gratification and "self-fulfillment." Even the word *relationship* can be expected to mean a temporary spell of sexual intimacy until the next one comes along. Marriages entered into within that ambient culture increasingly suffer from the same expectation. Divorce rates have soared over the decades (though in the United Kingdom they have declined recently), as have cohabitation without marriage, promiscuity generally, and abortion.

The deleterious impacts on the social fabric have also been well researched. Children suffer most, as they usually do. It is very hard to point to studies that suggest that children brought up by their two biological parents tend to thrive better on multiple metrics without being heard (and vilified for it) as condemning all single parents of either gender who may be parenting alone for all kinds of valid or understandable reasons.[13] That is not the point. The point would rather be that God's wisdom in building heterosexual marriage and families into his broad design for human society has been eroded at enormous cost for society's most vulnerable people, its children.

It is not just the human cost in broken, stunted, and lonely lives, though that in itself is a sad indictment of decades of sexual liberation and is another symptom of a disintegrating civilization. There is a massive and actual financial cost being borne by the public purse—the accumulated cost over the long term of all the collateral consequences of marriage and family breakdown. In the United Kingdom, the Marriage Foundation estimates the cost to the taxpayer of families splitting up across areas including tax, benefits, housing, health, social care, civil and criminal justice, and education as £51 billion. "Family breakdown is a social justice issue, with its appalling pain and distress, it's at an epidemic level and lies at the root of almost all society's problems. It particularly affects our children and it's the primary cause of inequality."[14]

Ecological devastation. We live in the midst of wanton destruction of God's creation, extinction of species, pollution of oceans and atmosphere, and the impact of climate breakdown as a result of accelerating (and feared near-irreversible) global warming. While these realities are not the exclusive fault of Europe and the United States alone, of course (some of the worst excesses of pollution, destruction, and emission of carbon dioxide are taking place in China, India, Brazil, Indonesia, etc.), the West certainly led the way in the factors that have exacerbated them and *could have* led the way in taking actions to mitigate them. In this case, the implications threaten not just Western civilization but potentially all human civilization on the planet.

As always, the poorest and most vulnerable of the world are already suffering the most.[15] Yet, we have known about global warming for a very long time. It was scientifically researched and understood nearly half a century ago by the very fossil-fuel companies that were contributing most to it—and then systematically denied by them. Doubts were repeatedly cast on the broad global scientific consensus that human activity (especially fossil-fuel burning) was contributing to it. Every sign of its obvious reality is dismissed as merely a freak weather phenomenon.[16] We seem willing even to sacrifice the future of the planet to the idol of short-term worship of Mammon.

The war on truth. In the shifting sands of postmodernity, truth is having a hard time. The suspicion that truth claims are little more than power plays has dug deep into popular consciousness and culture. "What's true for you is not necessarily true for me." Any claim that "your truth" must apply to me constitutes arrogance and judgmentalism (which has become a cardinal sin). But while such relativizing of the whole idea of truth is disturbing enough in itself at an intellectual and cultural level, and is ultimately corrosive of some of the foundations on which Western civilization was built (including science and technology), there is an even more sinister attack on truth in public life. That is the extent and normalizing of both quite deliberate and quite casual lying.

In recent years we seem to be living in the midst of a relentless war on truth at the highest levels. The ease with which lies are told by those in power (or those seeking it), and then simply shrugged off when the falsehood is exposed, with almost no accountability or consequences, is genuinely frightening in its implications for the survival of any kind of civic and political stability and public trust in government. In the sharp light of the Bible, this increasing trend is sinister and destructive, and by Jesus' standards, is satanic in origin (Jn 8:44).

What does it say about the state of our culture and politics that two men have risen to top political leadership in the United Kingdom and the United States who are both notoriously and demonstrably addicted to fabrication, exaggeration, false claims, self-contradiction, and downright mendacity? The danger is that the more it goes on, the longer it is tolerated or chuckled at ("Oh, that's just the way he is") or even applauded ("He tells it as he sees it"), the more it diminishes the values of honesty, trustworthiness, and integrity not only in public office but in all spheres of social and family life.

Indeed, what seems even more depressing and ominous is not merely that our political leaders so blatantly lie, shrug it off, and get away with it, but that so many ordinary people (if polls, vox pops, and focus groups are any indication) do not care. People have responded to journalists' questions in the United Kingdom by quite openly shrugging off the Prime Minister's lies with a response along the lines of "I don't care about the lies. I like him. He'll get things done." His attitude seems to be, "I know I'm lying. You know I'm lying. And I know that you know that I'm lying. But I don't care because you don't really either." That way, to be frank, lies chaos, or tyranny, or both in the end.

This combination of shameless lying by political leaders alongside complacent acceptance by the rest of the people drew astonished condemnation from Jeremiah, in words that resonate chillingly today.

> From the least to the greatest,
>> all are greedy for gain;
> prophets and priests alike,
>> all practice deceit.
> They dress the wound of my people
>> as though it were not serious.
> "Peace, peace," they say,
>> when there is no peace.
> *Are they ashamed of their detestable conduct?*
>> *No, they have no shame at all;*
>> *they do not even know how to blush.*
>>> (Jer 6:13-15 emphasis added)

> A horrible and shocking thing
>> has happened in the land:
> The prophets prophesy lies,
>> the priests rule by their own authority,
> and *my people love it this way.*
>> But what will you do in the end?
>>> (Jer 5:30-31 emphasis added)

In the United Kingdom, whatever side one took in the 2016 Brexit referendum, the greatest loser was truth, and along with it trust in any kind of evidence-based analysis or projection. Lies and false promises continued to be publicly repeated long after they had been thoroughly exposed as deliberately misleading. Meanwhile, social media facilitates the intentional dissemination of falsehoods and "fake news" (in the proper meaning of that phrase). People hear what they want to hear in the echo chambers of the algorithms that govern their smartphone screens.[17] All of this seems to accelerate a sad irony that Charles Spurgeon saw in his day, "A lie can travel half way round the world while the truth is putting on its boots."[18]

There is, as I said, something deeply satanic in this vicious attack on truth. It is increasing in scale, but its seriousness was already underlined in the Bible. Some of the harshest condemnations and laments in the Old Testament have to do with the loss of truth in the public arena (e.g., Ps 12:1-5; Amos 5:10). Could these words not be spoken with equally sharp relevance today?

> So justice is driven back,
>   and righteousness stands at a distance;
> *truth has stumbled in the streets,*
>   *honesty cannot enter.*
> *Truth is nowhere to be found,*
>   *and whoever shuns evil becomes a prey.* (Is 59:14-15
>   emphasis added)

That brings us back to the Bible, in the light of which we might find ourselves asking questions about the list of observations above—to which more could doubtless be added.

Can there be a sustainable future for a civilization and culture that is built on historic violence and bloodshed, that systemically increases poverty and inequality, that sets nation against nation, that corrodes the foundations of marriage and family, that desecrates God's creation, and that devalues to the point of meaningless the very concept of public truth? Given that all of these symptoms of human fallenness receive severe condemnation in the Bible, do we not hear the Judge of all the earth saying to the Western world, "Enough is enough"?

As I try to answer such questions biblically, I find myself going to the book of Judges. There we see a story of increasing social fragmentation and violence, with accelerating social decline, tribal wars, and acts of frightening moral depravity, including sexual violence and mass murders. The same kind of questions arise.

How could it have happened, we ask ourselves, that a nation that had been so blessed by God with deliverance from slavery and persecution (which it celebrated annually in the thanksgiving feast of Passover), a nation gifted with a fertile land of its own, a nation established on the basis of a constitution of rights and responsibilities (which we call the law of Moses, especially Deuteronomy)—how could such a blessed and privileged people fall into such utterly dysfunctional disintegration over a few generations and thereby repeatedly incur God's judgment? How indeed! Yet they did, and Paul tells us these narratives were written down for our learning (1 Cor 10:1-11).

To see what we can learn, we need to spend some time in our next chapter thinking about what the Bible tells us about God's desire for social, economic, and political life, its analysis of the idols that frustrate God's plan for human flourishing, and its portrayal of God's judgment at work within history.

The Bible has a lot more to teach us about that realm of public life than many people think—especially if they never read the Old Testament. There is a remarkably rich and comprehensive political, economic, and social theology and ethic in the Bible, which Western Christianity has pretty well ignored for centuries.[19]

CHAPTER SIX

GOD IN THE POLITICAL ARENA

THE GOD OF OLD TESTAMENT Israel showed himself passionately concerned about the political life of his people. He provided multiple laws *to govern those who governed*, and he sent the prophets to challenge and correct them when needed. In this chapter, we will look first at how the Bible makes very clear the standards God requires of those in political office; then at how it exposes the idols that God rejects, which easily infest public life; and finally at how it portrays the judgment that God operates within history, when whole societies persist in rejecting those standards and instead pursue those idols.

As we begin, remember the point I made in chapter five on how part of God's intention for Israel was not only to be the vehicle by which God's redemptive blessing would reach all nations, but also to function as a model or paradigm, embodying principles that reflect God's desires and demands across the international spectrum of nations, cultures, and history.

The Bible reveals the standards that God requires in public life

Here are just three examples of the values and standards that God holds up for the behavior of those in public office. Many more could be listed.[1]

1. Modesty: The law of the king (Deut 17:14-20). God did not command Israel to have a king. But, in the event that it might decide to adopt that form of government, God did instruct it on what kind of king the people should seek to appoint. Basically, the king in Israel was to be unlike any king they might have known.

Israel's king was not to be like the monarchies of surrounding cultures, which built their political authority on spectacular extravagance of wealth and all the trappings of military power and greed. Not so in Israel. "The king, moreover, must not acquire great numbers of horses for himself or make the people return to Egypt to get more of them, for the LORD has told you, 'You are not to go back that way again.' He must not take many wives, or his heart will be led astray. He must not accumulate large amounts of silver and gold" (Deut 17:16-17). God's law put a prohibition on weapons (horses/chariots), harems, and excessive silver and gold. A king in Israel (and all the government apparatus that would surround him) was *not* to be characterized by the classic trio: *money, sex, and power.*

All three standards were broken by Solomon, of course, and most of the kings in Judah and Israel who followed him. Such standards have been flouted by many political and religious leaders ever since. Indeed, all three of those things that were prohibited to kings among God's people are the very things that today's political leaders openly boast about, with impunity—especially sexual profligacy and excessive wealth. We are ruled by millionaires and billionaires whose political office serves to increase their already phenomenal wealth.

God intended a very different kind of politics.

2. Integrity: Accountability in public office (1 Sam 12:1-5). In between the era of the tribal judges and the emergence of monarchy stands the towering figure of Samuel. He was the last of the judges, and in some ways he functioned almost like the first king. He exercised a position of national leadership throughout his lifetime in judicial, military, and political affairs.

At the close of his life, after Saul has been appointed as king and Samuel is about to step down as the leader of the people, Samuel takes a very significant step. He opens the books and makes himself accountable to the people. His words constitute an invitation for an audit of his tenure of office. He calls on the people as witnesses and God as judge. He is open for inspection. He claims that he has acted with integrity, but he submits that claim to public accountability. In fact, Samuel's accountability is a key factor in his integrity.

> Samuel said to all Israel, "I have listened to everything you said to me and have set a king over you. Now you have a king as your leader. As for me, I am old and gray, and my sons are here with you. I have been your leader from my youth until this day. Here I stand. Testify against me in the presence of the LORD and his anointed. Whose ox have I taken? Whose donkey have I taken? Whom have I cheated? Whom have I oppressed? From whose hand have I accepted a bribe to make me shut my eyes? If I have done any of these things, I will make it right."
>
> "You have not cheated or oppressed us," they replied. "You have not taken anything from anyone's hand."
>
> Samuel said to them, "The LORD is witness against you, and also his anointed is witness this day, that you have not found anything in my hand."
>
> "He is witness," they said. (1 Sam 12:1-5)

This is a revealing account. Specifically, Samuel claims (1) that he had not profited from public office for personal gain and (2) that he had not betrayed public trust by corruption and bribery. The people accept and affirm his claim. He has discharged his public office with integrity and honesty.

Those are key standards for anybody in political life and leadership. They would still be held up, of course, as ideals in our own political realm. They are supposed to be protected by constitutional restrictions, emoluments clauses, avoidance of conflict of interest, and other forms of legal sanction. The principles go back a long way, and Samuel's simple words express them within the culture of Israel at that time. Those who are in positions of power must be transparently accountable and submit their integrity to public scrutiny.

Samuel also warns the people (in 1 Sam 8:10-20) that the kings they want to have ruling them will do the very things that Samuel says he has not done. Read his powerful speech in 1 Samuel 8:10-20. Kings will twist the whole political and economic system to the advantage and enrichment of themselves and their cronies. There will be taxation, military conscription, confiscation of land, forced labor for the king's benefit, and so on. The ordinary people will end up feeling enslaved as they pay a heavy price for their political leaders—kings in Israel, and their many equivalents in our modern cultures. Samuel was absolutely right about the way Israel's monarchy would behave in the centuries to follow.

Samuel's warnings still ring true today. Ordinary people pay a very heavy price for the venality and self-seeking of those in political office. Accountability and integrity sometimes seem more honored in the breach than in practice.

3. Justice: God's fundamental demand (Prov 31:3, 8-9, etc.). God's criterion for the moral evaluation of government is the extent to which those in power exercise the power entrusted to them on behalf of the *powerless* and ensure justice for the poor, oppressed, and exploited, including the foreigner. The latter (foreigners, immigrants) are particularly prominent in Old Testament law as needing protection and justice. "Love them [the foreigner] as yourself" balances "Love your neighbor as yourself" (Lev 19:18, 34).

The requirement of doing justice, as the primary function of political leadership, is ubiquitous in the Old Testament. King Lemuel's mother sums it up in her wise advice to her son (a text sadly ignored as we rush on to the praise of the wonderful wife in the rest of the chapter):

The sayings of King Lemuel—an inspired utterance his mother taught him.

Listen, my son! Listen, son of my womb!

Listen, my son, the answer to my prayers!

Do not spend your strength on women,
your vigor on those who ruin kings.

It is not for kings, Lemuel—

> it is not for kings to drink wine,
>> not for rulers to crave beer,
> lest they drink and forget what has been decreed,
>> and deprive all the oppressed of their rights. . . .
>
> *Speak up for those who cannot speak for themselves,*
>> *for the rights of all who are destitute.*
> *Speak up and judge fairly;*
>> *defend the rights of the poor and needy.* (Prov 31:1-5, 8-9
>> emphasis added)

David's repeated prayer for Solomon is that he should do justice for his people (Ps 72:1-2, 12-14). It is also Solomon's prayer for himself, though sadly he departs far from it later in his reign (1 Kings 3:9-12).

Jeremiah holds up God's standards of justice as the criteria for legitimacy for the Davidic monarchy itself. Failure to follow God's ways by ensuring social justice will bring the nation down and the king with it.

> This is what the LORD says: "Go down to the palace of the king of Judah and proclaim this message there: 'Hear the word of the LORD to you, king of Judah, you who sit on David's throne—you, your officials and your people who come through these gates. This is what the LORD says: Do what is just and right. Rescue from the hand of the oppressor the one who has been robbed. Do no wrong or violence to the foreigner, the fatherless or the widow, and do not shed innocent blood in this place. For if you are careful to carry out these commands, then kings who sit on David's throne will come through the gates of this palace, riding in chariots and on horses, accompanied by their officials and their people. But if you do not obey these commands, declares the LORD, I swear by myself that this palace will become a ruin.'" (Jer 22:1-5)

Jeremiah's specific target at that time was the manifest greedy and unjust opulence of King Jehoiakim, which he contrasts with the godly justice of Josiah. Pointedly, Jeremiah affirms that doing justice is definitive of knowing God (Jer 22:13-17).

Amos, of course, puts it most memorably in the context of the rampant social injustice of his day, with God's demand to "Let justice roll on like a river, righteousness like a never failing stream!" (Amos 5:24) matched perhaps by Micah's equally memorable triplet:

He has shown you, O mortal, what is good.
    And what does the LORD require of you?
To act justly and to love mercy
    and to walk humbly with your God. (Mic 6:8)

So then, across the whole range of the Old Testament canon, in the Law, the Prophets, and the Writings, we find these core values at the heart of the way God wanted public affairs and political leadership to be exercised: with modesty, integrity, and justice.

The Bible exposes the idols that God rejects

As we surveyed in part one, idolatry is a very important topic in the Bible—much neglected by contemporary evangelical Christians, partly because we ourselves are unconsciously involved with and sometimes dominated by the false gods of the people around us (like Old Testament Israel). Indeed, I believe that one reason for the slow but accelerating collapse of Western civilization is the profoundly syncretistic and idolatrous nature of Western Christianity, combined with the idolatry of the culture that surrounds us. We, God's people, like Israel of old, are in uncritical collusion with the false gods of our ambient cultures.

The threat of false gods loomed large in God's preparation of Israel for moving into the land of Canaan. Read, for example, the serious and prolonged warning of Deuteronomy 4:15-31. Its message is simple: at all costs, avoid idolatry! The critique of idolatry in the Old Testament, however, was far more than merely a prohibition on making physical statues of alleged gods, or on the worship of created objects (sun, moon, stars, creatures, earth itself).

As we saw in some detail in part one, the Old Testament affirms that all false gods are, in the final analysis, "the work of human hands" (that is the commonest charge made against them). What that means is not just that the statues are carved by hand (as everybody knew) but also that *the gods they are alleged to represent* are nothing but human constructs. We create our own gods out of the things that entice us (prestige, glory, wealth), or to ward off things we fear (disease, enemies, bad weather), or to give us the things we need (crops, fertility, rain, survival beyond death). We exchange the worship of the living Creator God, who deals with all these matters for us according to his own providence and will, for whatever we can construct and put in his place for our own happiness and security. Because all such gods are the work of our own hands, even when they harness forces of demonic evil within themselves, they cannot deliver what we hope for. False gods fail. That is the only thing we can be sure of.

There are all kinds of false gods and idols in human cultures, but in relation to Old Testament Israel's social, economic, and political life, three could be highlighted as particularly toxic and destructive, especially as they enticed those in political power—kings and governments—All three have their modern manifestations all around us in Western culture. These are still the gods of our culture, but here seen through the lens of the Old Testament.

1. The idol of prosperity. In Canaanite culture and religion, Baal was the god of sex and fertility (human, animal, and crops), the god of business deals and money, the god of the revolving seasons and their life-giving potential, the god of the land itself. . . . Baal seems to have been god of everything that mattered in everyday life. The temptation that the Israelites faced must have seemed overwhelmingly plausible. If you want to be successful and prosperous in this land, you need to follow the ways of the god of the people who already live and prosper there (or gods—since there were multiple baals as manifestations of the god Baal, son of the high god, El). Of course, you could keep Yahweh for national identity (he was the God of Israel). Yahweh would still be the national God who could be counted on to bless the country (whatever that means). Yahweh, after all, is a great God to have for Sabbath days and festivals, or in battles. But for the rest of life? Then you need Baal—for health and wealth.

The prophets fought a centuries-long battle against this tendency of preexilic Israel to go after the baals of the land in ways that involved ritual prostitution (for fertility) and attributing all the blessings of creation to Baal, rather than to their true Giver, Yahweh God.

But this was not merely a religious matter—as if it were simply about which god you worship on the Sabbath or at the local shrine. The kind of society that Yahweh's laws created and sustained stood in stark contrast to the kind of social, economic, and political culture where Baal reigned. The narrative of Naboth, Ahab, and Jezebel illustrates this graphically (1 Kings 21).

When King Ahab offers to buy Naboth's vineyard or exchange some land for it, Naboth recoils in shock. Land, under Israel's law, could not simply be bought and sold but had to remain with the line of family inheritance for the long-term well-being of smaller household units (Lev 25:23). Ahab's request is illegal, and he knows it. So he just sulks.

Jezebel, on the other hand, came from Phoenicia. She was the ardent advocate of establishing the worship of Baal in Israel and extirpating the worship of Yahweh. Her politics were radically different. Where she came from, a king could have or take what he wanted. So she uses Israel's own laws to arrange for the judicial murder of Naboth and his sons, leaving his property vacant with no heir. She then hands it on a plate to her husband. In other words, the idolatry of Baal went hand in hand with the increasing social and economic evils of oppression and dispossession. By the next century, the fate of Naboth seems to have become so commonplace that all the eighth-century prophets condemn the increasing dispossession of the poor.

Idolatry and injustice rode in tandem in Israel. They still do. Yahweh alone is the God of justice. Yahweh is the God who takes the side of the Naboths of the world and sends Elijah to condemn Ahab's government for its rapacity, cruelty, and greed. Baal is the god who fosters and even glorifies the practices of the powerful that lead to the suffering and dispossession of the weak. The idolatry of Mammon still drives the impoverishment of those who get in the way.

The worship of Baal is alive and well in Western culture—with our idolizing of sex and money. As the Canaanites (and Israel after them) worshiped fertility in its broadest sense, so we worship its modern equivalents. We must have an abundance of everything. Consumerism as an ideology feeds the economy, which in turn depends on creating insatiable consumer demand and unpayable consumer debt.

Then, to the idolatry of consumerism we add the idolatry of celebrity. Superwealth goes with glamour, fame, and an extravagant lifestyle (not always, of course). The combined idols of money and celebrity tend to blind us to the uncomfortable facts that the exorbitant wealth of very few is at the expense of, or at least certainly flaunted alongside, the abject poverty of many, and that the wealthiest 0.01 percent tend to contribute very little to the common good—certainly nothing proportionate to their wealth.[2]

Then we go further and assume that someone who has achieved great wealth and celebrity must, for those reasons alone, have the wisdom and expertise to give trusted advice on many other areas of life. We consume their opinions and words with awe. We deem them worthy of political leadership. Wealth generates respect, deserved or otherwise. We exalt those who seem to embody the gods we worship ourselves.

Job recognized that worshiping money was as much a form of idolatry as worshiping the heavenly bodies, and just as sinful in the eyes of the living God.

> If I have put my trust in gold
>   or said to pure gold, "You are my security,"
> if I have rejoiced over my great wealth,
>   the fortune my hands had gained,
> if I have regarded the sun in its radiance
>   or the moon moving in splendor,
> so that my heart was secretly enticed
>   and my hand offered them a kiss of homage,

then these also would be sins to be judged,
    for I would have been unfaithful to God on high.
      (Job 31:24-28)

Jesus and the New Testament call the worship of wealth "Mammon." It still dominates our culture in so many ways. In the United States especially, and the United Kingdom increasingly, extreme wealth has massive influence on our politics. We get the best government that money can buy (through the astronomical sums spent in elections), and then we get the policies and actions that corporate interests and billionaire lobbyists can extract for party contributions and other favors. Western democracies are morphing into plutocracies.[3]

But because most of us in the general population, Christian or not, are in one way or another participants in the worship of Mammon, the system goes on perpetuating the corruption, injustice, and suffering that false gods trail in their wake. Indeed, some Christians cash in on the idolatry of the culture around them by simply baptizing it into the practice of their religion—in the unbiblical deception that calls itself the prosperity gospel. As I write elsewhere, in a world where Mammon is god, the name of the living God himself can be enlisted to serve Mammon, as the charlatans of the church in every age have proved, form Tetzel selling his indulgences for buying forgiveness in the sixteenth century to televangelists selling salvation, healing, and prosperity today.[4]

2. The idol of national pride. As we saw in the introduction to part two, there is a revealing story in 1 Kings 12. Jeroboam had led ten of the tribes of Israel into secession from the government in Jerusalem under King Rehoboam. Rehoboam had perpetuated and aggravated the oppressive policies of the later years of the reign of his father Solomon. Jeroboam led the rebellion against him and established himself as king of the new northern state that took the name Israel for itself. He became King Jeroboam I. Then, in order to bolster his own kingdom and its security, Jeroboam fabricated gods—two bull-calf statues at either end of his kingdom. He echoed Aaron (Ex 32:1-6) in claiming that these gods somehow represented Yahweh, who brought Israel out of Egypt. But the idolatrous dimension is very clear: he created shrines for them and devised festivals and priests of his own choosing to serve them (1 Kings 12:26-33).

In other words, this was a national cultural religion, to establish the pride and image of his own kingdom as over against his rival, Judah. He was using God to serve the security of his own state. Rather than leading his people in the service and worship of the living God, in obedience to the standards of covenant law, he blatantly used the name and symbols of the God of Israel to bless and glorify the state and the political establishment that he himself had set up.

So it is not surprising that when Amos comes to preach in the northern kingdom a century later, during the reign of Jeroboam II, condemning the nation for the social and economic injustice that is rampant, he is told to get out and go home by Amaziah, the chief priest of the sanctuary at Bethel, with these revealing words: "Get out, you seer! Go back to the land of Judah. Earn your bread there and do your prophesying there. Don't prophesy anymore at Bethel, because this is *the king's sanctuary and the temple of the kingdom*" (Amos 7:12-13 emphasis added).

The sanctuary and the temple were now serving the interests of the state, not the covenant demands of the Lord God. Religion was co-opted to serve the national interest.

Later, the kings of Judah idolized the gods of Assyria, even bringing their statues into the temple. This may have been forced on them, as a vassal state. Nevertheless, one gets the impression that Kings Ahaz and Manasseh *admired* the power of Assyria's empire. The Assyrians were ruthless, they were smart, they were great, they knew how to conquer and rule. So if you want to be great, get with them! The result of this idolatry of national status—sought or bought—was increasing social evil, domestic violence, massive loss of national treasure in tribute paid to Assyria, absurd posturings on the international stage between Assyria, Egypt, and Babylon, and the cost of military expeditions and needless alliances and conflicts.

In the end both kingdoms, Israel and Judah, paid the price for their nationalistic idolatries. Seeking to make a great name for themselves (the original sin of Babel), they ignored the promise of God to Abraham that God would make his people great. Seeking to bolster their own security, they failed to trust the promise of the prophets that Yahweh alone was all the security they needed.

One particular form that this idolatry of national greatness takes is the obsession with military security (as we see in the reign of Solomon and subsequent kings) and the hero worship of the military itself. It is not just the amount of a nation's wealth that is spent on military defense—though that can reach staggering proportions.[5] It is not just that we have begun to mimic nations that engage in spectacularly boastful displays of military hardware and massed human forces. It is the willingness of Christian churches to seemingly sanctify and baptize emblems of national pride and the military virulence of the state that I find syncretistic.

In the United Kingdom, many historic churches have military emblems and regimental flags displayed, sometimes alongside the Communion table. I have said before that I do not reject legitimate patriotism within biblical limits, but what message is conveyed by imperial symbols of war beside the heartbeat of the gospel of the self-sacrifice of the Prince of Peace? In the United States many churches prominently fly the Stars and Stripes. In one church, I stood as the national flag was processed into the church at the start of the service along with the Bible and the holy sacraments. Again, what is someone committed to the exclusive worship of the living God to make of this conflation? At the very least, to an outsider again, it seems ironic given the stringent constitutional separation of church and state. Peter tells Christians to honor the emperor, and Paul tells them to pay their taxes. But it is hard to imagine early Christians gathering for worship around symbols of the Roman empire or its regimental eagles.

In ancient pantheons, there were greater national gods and subordinate gods in kinship relationships. The same phenomenon might be reflected in the way the idolatry of *national* security in the United States seems to go hand in hand (literally) with the proliferation of guns in private hands, allegedly for *personal* security. To outside observers like me, the gun is surely in the Olympian superleague of American gods. It reigns over all its opponents and defeats every attempt to restrict its sovereignty. The gun-god exacts the most horrific sacrifices of human lifeblood—child sacrifice no less—and shrugs off every wave of revulsion that follows such events.[6] Those who defend this god seem characteristically to be devoted worshipers of the god of national greatness also, symbolized by the flag. Frequently both (guns and patriotism, along with the Second Amendment) are harnessed to the name of God, in a form of syncretism that I find virtually blasphemous. You can get T-shirts and other paraphernalia emblazoned with the astounding opinion that "God, guns, and guts made America free (or great); let's keep all three." I have seen them in regular grocery and hardware stores, and advertised online as "just the thing for conservative Christians."[7]

3. The idol of self-exaltation. This can be a very personal idol. It goes right back to the fall, when the first humans created in God's image chose the path of moral autonomy. They chose to distrust God's goodness, reject God's authority, and disobey God's instructions. They succumbed to the satanic lie that we humans could put ourselves in the place of God. Not content to be made in the image of God, they chose to usurp the domain of God and be the arbiters of good and evil for themselves.

The profoundly simple narrative of Genesis 3 portrays in graphic imagery a momentous historical turn in human history and also captures the very essence of the sin we continue to commit ever since. It is for good reason, then, that pride is listed as the first of the traditional seven deadly sins. It is the idolatry of the self.

But this idolatry of the self also afflicts whole cultures and nations. The positive value of rugged self-reliance easily morphs into the vice of self-worship and narcissism. Relentless and quite shameless narcissism has become characteristic of Western culture. Indeed, in a popular form it has become a virtue, fed by the advertising industry. "You owe it to yourself." "Because you're worth it." "Believe in yourself." The slogans of our culture get into the bloodstream of children from a very early age. The message of successive Disney movies is that you can be whatever you want to be. You just have to believe in yourself. Some of our leaders never seem to leave that childhood stage of narcissism verging on ego-centric megalomania.

Isaiah saw right through that kind of self-exalting, self-defending arrogance and called it out for the sheer idolatry that it truly is when whole societies and their rulers succumb to it. Note the reference to the idols at the end.

> The LORD Almighty has a day in store
> for all the proud and lofty,
> for all that is exalted
> (and they will be humbled), . . .
> The arrogance of man will be brought low
> and human pride humbled;
> the LORD alone will be exalted in that day,
> and the idols will totally disappear. (Is 2:12, 17-18)

We have already seen how Ezekiel identifies self-importance as the primary idolatry of the great trading nation of Tyre and the great empire of Egypt, and exposes the vaunting, mad arrogance of these rulers in their wealth and power (Ezek 28:2-5; 29:2-3).

There are many more gods and idols in popular and political culture, of course. The story of Israel in the Old Testament is the story of one great long struggle between Yahweh the living God, the Creator and Redeemer, holy and just, true and good—and the idols that constantly threatened and tempted Israel, idols that are still lurking in our Western cultures and increasingly dominate our politics, with such damaging and corrupting power.[8]

So far in this chapter, then, we have seen that the Bible reveals the standards that God requires and exposes the idols that God rejects. But the Bible does more; it also warns us of the terrible *price* that such idolatry demands in the end. False gods always cost you in the end.

The cost of idolatry is the outworking of God's judgment.

The Bible discerns the judgment that God operates within history

As we saw, the book of Judges portrays a downward spiral, as repeated idolatry results in national decline, fragmentation, increasing violence, moral depravity, and eventual anarchy. The explanation toward the end of the book is that "every one did what was right in his own eyes" and "there was no king in Israel." That last statement has a double resonance. On the one hand, it implies that the people have rejected Yahweh as their true king. They are failing to live by the covenantal standards he gave them, and their national disobedience to God's rule is creating the social chaos that God indeed warned them about.

On the other hand, of course, "there was no king in Israel" is a statement of simple fact at a human level. The Israelites were living as a loose federation of tribes with leaders (judges) raised up by God as needs arose. But as the chaos and mayhem increased, a statement such as "there was no king in Israel" seems to imply that perhaps, if only they could get a really strong human king ("like all the other nations"), then that would solve the problems of idolatry, social fracturing, and insecurity.

When times are chaotic and threatening, you need a strong man—a no-nonsense authoritarian leader who will get things done and fix all the problems. That is precisely the circumstances that have brought authoritarian demagogues to power in the Philippines and Brazil, for example, just as it is the justification that many, including many Christians, use for supporting their excessive use of extrajudicial force and dictatorial tendencies.

So will Israel getting a king solve the problems of the book of Judges? Along comes the monarchy in the next two books of the Bible, and after a shaky start (Saul), the nation seems to do well (for a while), under David and the early reign of Solomon. But then? Within a generation, the cycle begins to repeat: kings and people are found breaking all the standards God required, going after all the idols God rejected, and reaping the judgment that God had threatened. Far from solving the problems of the book of Judges, these strong leaders (kings) mostly make things a lot worse.

In the Hebrew canon, the books of Samuel and Kings are among the Former Prophets. That means that the writers and editors of these narratives (from Joshua to 2 Kings) interpret the history of the monarchy in Israel from a prophetic perspective; *they see things as God saw them.* When these narrative texts are set alongside the books of the Latter Prophets (Isaiah, Jeremiah, Ezekiel, and the Book of the Twelve), they show very clearly how the people of Israel go from one degree of idolatry to another, generation after generation, *led by their rulers.* Successive governments fail to halt the slide—with very few exceptions (Jehoshaphat, Hezekiah, and Josiah). Ignoring the warnings of the prophets that such behavior will inevitably bring total disaster on the whole nation, they go on spiraling downward. These books tell the convoluted and depressing—but very revealing—story of moral, spiritual, and national collapse. Both kingdoms, Israel and Judah, pursue their idolatrous paths combined with rampant social and economic injustice, and judicial and political corruption, until in the end God lets their chosen direction take them to its inevitable destination—death and destruction.

What were the symptoms? What was happening in this process? How can we learn from it?

The biblical historical record and the prophetic commentary highlight a number of factors that contributed to God's judgment, operating within the processes of national decay. All of these continue as lethal toxins within contemporary politics:

- increasing economic disparity, with wealth accumulating in fewer hands and multitudes being reduced to poverty, dispossession, and homelessness—especially the most vulnerable, that is, women and children (Is 5:8; Mic 2:1-2);

- corruption of the political system, through government favors, cronyism, nepotism, and patronage (1 Sam 8);
- corruption of the judicial system, through control of the courts by the wealthy, and widespread bribery (Amos);
- increase in violence, bloodshed, political murders (Is 1; Ezek 22);
- widespread and religiously approved sexual promiscuity (Hosea); and
- a whole culture of lies, denial, moral confusion, and shameless inability even to blush (Jer 2; 5; 6).

Now, it is important to understand that these lurid factors of Israel's political and economic life were not something *separate* from its religious unfaithfulness to Yahweh its God (idolatry). Rather, these social phenomena were the evidence and outworking of its national idolatries. When you worship false gods—the kind of idols we identified above and many others—then this is what happens in society. When the whole community refuses to walk in the ways of Yahweh—the God of justice, integrity, truth, and compassion—and deliberately chooses the way of the gods of greed, sex, fertility, personal, and national pride, then the whole society becomes permeated with corruption, inequality, oppression, lies, and violence.

Until, in the end, after centuries of prophetic warnings and divine patience, *God gives them up to the inevitable operation of his moral judgment.* As Ezekiel and Jeremiah put it: How could God do otherwise than bring his judgment on such a depraved society, a society that was behaving even worse than the Canaanites they had driven out centuries earlier or the nations that surrounded them?

So the nation collapsed, corroded from within and attacked from without, into virtual extinction in the Babylonian exile. The destruction of Jerusalem and the exile to Babylon was the most traumatic event in the history of Old Testament Israel. It is portrayed, unambiguously, by the prophets as at one and the same time the outworking of *God's judgment,* mediated through the *geopolitical and military realities* of their day. The book of Lamentations leaves us shuddering at the cost the whole society paid for the sin and folly primarily of its leaders. Just reading it brings tears to the eyes. How terribly the ordinary people of Israel suffered because of the endemic and perpetual sin and idolatry into which their rulers had led them. Their worship of false gods, manifested in social, economic, and political policies and practices, rebounded on their own heads in national implosion and collapse, through events in which the prophets discerned the hand of God's judgment.

That should have been the end for Israel. Indeed, it *would have been* the end, had it not been for the grace and long-term missional goal and promises of God—that through this people Israel, God planned to bring blessing to all nations on earth. So, just as God had remembered his covenant with Abraham when the Israelites were in Egypt, so God again acted to redeem and restore his people from exile in Babylon. Approximately two generations after the destruction of Jerusalem in 587 BC, Israel was restored to its land under the edict of the Persian emperor Cyrus, in 538 BC.

But the point we need to make is this. This Old Testament cycle of endemic and repeated idolatry, leading to ever-increasing social dissolution and eventually to total national collapse, is also "written for our learning." It was, at one level, unique as the history of the covenant people, Old Testament Israel. But at another level, Israel embodied and lived out the *sins of humanity* itself. As a nation among the nations, Israel was tempted to go the way of the nations, and—but for the grace and mission of God—they would indeed have suffered the ultimate fate of so many other nations: that is, extinction.

The story of Israel is a centuries-long case study in the growth and the costs of national idolatry and the outworking of God's judgment through the down-to-earth realities of social, economic, political, and international affairs. This is what happens, it cries out to us, when people abandon the worship and ways of the living God and let the idols rule over them.

Be warned! says Paul, writing to Christians about the dangers of infidelity to the God of our salvation (1 Cor 10). But the warning applies more widely than to the Christian church only. My argument in this second part of the book, and indeed the reason for the in-depth study of the first part, is based on the strong hermeneutical conviction that Old Testament Israel was intended by God neither as a self-contained people redeemed and covenanted for their own exclusive benefit nor merely as a quarry for spiritual lessons that could be applied to the church in the New Testament and resource Christian preachers ever since. There is not space to develop the argument fully here, but the point is that Israel, according to many texts, was created by God not only to be the vehicle by which his redemptive blessing and covenant relationship would spread to people from all nations on earth, but also to be shaped through its Torah to be a model of what a society governed by the character and demands of Yahweh God should look like.[9] Accordingly, there are principles embodied and worked out within Israel's laws and Israel's history from which God *intended* us to learn how human life in the social arena might flourish best and to learn, negatively, the kinds of behaviors that prove ultimately destructive of human welfare in so many realms.

Conclusion

But as human beings, whether Israelites or the other nations, whether (in New Testament terms) Jews or Gentiles, we have failed to pay heed to the living God and chosen the way of idolatry—to our own massive cost. *That is precisely how Paul interprets the human predicament in Romans 1.* Paul's portrayal of the universality of human sin draws heavily on the Old Testament Scriptures (just as his theology of salvation also starts with Abraham). He makes it very clear: when human beings (individuals, nations, whole cultures) persist in following idols, in the end God gives them up to what they want and what they worship.

God's judgment works itself out in the kind of social disintegration that Paul describes. The horrible social evils that Paul lists are not so much the *reasons* for God's judgment (though of course, as sinful behavior, they do stand under God's judgment) as rather the *content and experience* of God's judgment in the present (without denying, of course, the eschatological reality of God's final judgment). Here is what society becomes, with all the suffering that such practices generate, when God gives us up to our own idolatry and choices.

> Just as they did not think it worthwhile to retain the knowledge of God, so God gave them over to a depraved mind, so that they do what ought not to be done. They have become filled with every kind of wickedness, evil, greed and depravity. They are full of envy, murder, strife, deceit and malice. They are gossips, slanderers, God-haters, insolent, arrogant and boastful; they invent ways of doing evil; they disobey their parents; they have no understanding, no fidelity, no love, no mercy. Although they know God's righteous decree that those who do such things deserve death, they not only continue to do these very things but also approve of those who practice them. (Rom 1:28-32)

In the end, when you submit to the idols (as Western cultures have been doing now for centuries), the idols will eventually come to rule over you. We are reaping what we have been sowing for generations. "Here are your gods . . . !" says God. "You chose them. You adore them. You sacrifice to them. You live with the consequences."

That, I think, is what the events of 2016, Brexit and the US presidential election, with all their chaotic results in the social and political life of both nations over recent years, are *symptomatic* of. They seem to be an outcome of long-term idolatry and short-term folly. They seem to be both the epitome and intensification of cultural and social idolatrous trends.

Perhaps they will play some part, in God's sovereign governance of the history of nations, in the outworking of God's principles of judgment on Western cultures. Only God knows whether that is so. All I can say, with no prophetic credentials, is that they seem to be symptomatic of a whole civilization in deep and possibly irreversible trouble. God's judgment simply gives us up to the gods we choose. It is sometimes said, "You get the government you deserve." The Bible would retort, "And you get the gods you worship." The history of Israel shows that the two are very closely related. You get the government that mirrors the gods you worship.

The idols have come to rule. The idols of wealth, sex, guns, race, nationalism, and self-love have found their incarnation.

In the end, God says, "Here is your king, O Israel." This is what you asked for, this is what you get. The principles of *God's* judgment work themselves out in the realities of *humanly* chosen ends and means, *human* decisions and directions, *human* failures and follies.

The Greeks had a saying, attributed to one of their poets, "Those whom the gods wish to destroy, they first make mad." John Calvin, with greater biblical intuition from his immersion in the Old Testament Scriptures, stated that when God puts a nation under judgment, he gives it wicked leaders.[10]

How then should we live in such a world as this? To that question we now turn.

Part three

GOD'S PEOPLE IN AN IDOLATROUS WORLD

WHAT DOES IT MEAN to be the people of God in the midst of the kind of idolatries we have sketched in part two? What is required of us? The first thing, surely, has to be that we turn away from the multiple false gods that so easily infect our own Christian lives, seeping insidiously into our subconscious minds from the ambient culture and return to the one true living God of the Bible. That is not just a single moment that happens at conversion. In fact, it only begins then. It has to become a lifetime's habit in which we intentionally recognize and reject the idols and deliberately and persistently choose the living God instead. Indeed, I would suggest that the older we get the more we need to remind ourselves to keep doing this. "Choose for yourselves *this day* whom you will serve, whether the gods your ancestors served beyond the Euphrates, or the gods of the Amorites, in whose land you are living. But as for me and my household, we will serve the Lord" (Josh 24:15).

Joshua threw out this challenge to the people of Israel when he himself was "by then a very old man" (Josh 23:1), and the people he was addressing had lived through that whole generation of the conquest of Canaan. It was a challenge to go on *choosing* to serve Yahweh, the one living God, and to *keep on refusing* to serve the old gods or the new ones they would soon encounter.

But surely, they might have responded, "Our parents chose to serve Yahweh back at Mount Sinai in the wilderness." "That's not enough," Joshua might have replied, thinking of the rest of the wilderness story. Surely, they might have persisted, "*We* chose to serve Yahweh as we entered this land and defeated our enemies." "That's not enough either," Joshua would insist. The false gods of those enemies were still all around them, promising agricultural success, sexual fertility, and all the other good things of this new land. No, there had to be a deliberate, covenantally sealed choice—again and again. "Choose *this day* whom you will serve."

That is a challenge that echoes and re-echoes through the Scriptures, from the prophets to the last verse of 1 John. It is the call to *radical God-centered living*. What could such a call mean for us? That is what we explore in part three.

In chapter 7 we shall look at three dimensions of such God-centeredness: shaping our lives by the *story* of God, participating in the *mission* of God, and seeking the *kingdom* of God. In our final chapter, we shall consider some of the ethical and spiritual implications of such God-centeredness in lives that are distinctive from the world around us and in the practice of prayer that is shaped by the prayers of the Bible itself.

CHAPTER SEVEN

A PEOPLE SHAPED
BY THE LIVING GOD

L IVING AS GOD'S PEOPLE in the midst of a fallen world is the great challenge that has faced the people God called to be his own ever since our beginnings in the loins and womb of Abraham and Sarah, all through the centuries of Old Testament Israel, and the history of the Christian church. It has so many dimensions and demands. But among them must come at least these three: we are people shaped by the word of God, sharing in the mission of God, and living under the kingdom of God. Let's think what each of these should mean for us today.

We must be Bible people: living by the story of God

Doubtless, if we are Christians we probably would claim to be Bible people already. But what do we think the Bible actually is? One way to interpret how Christians view the Bible is to notice how they mostly use it.

For some, the Bible is a book of rules—a toolkit for morally upright living. They use the Bible mainly as an ethical guidebook, by which they claim to live their own lives, teach others how to live theirs, and where necessary condemn those who fall short of the Bible's standards. We've done some of that already in this book.

For some, the Bible is a book of promises—a reservoir of encouraging thoughts for each day. They like to have Bible verses around the home, printed on attractive scenes and framed, or embedded in beautiful memes for sharing on social media. They find comfort, hope, and peace, in those verses that speak of all three.

For some, the Bible is a book of doctrines—the raw material for building dogmatic systems of theology. They are serious about the Christian faith and have a didactic frame of mind. They nourish themselves on books of sound theology that strongly emphasize the biblical texts that support each major doctrine, and equally the biblical texts that refute all kinds of false doctrines.

Now, the Bible certainly includes plenty of all of these—clear ethical standards, wonderfully comforting promises, and robust theological truths. But in the form that God has providentially given his Word to us, its overall canonical shape, the Bible is fundamentally a story—or rather *the* Story, the story of God, the universe, and everything, including the history and future of our world. It has a wonderfully good beginning, a massive invading and threatening problem that is addressed and finally resolved through its vast and complex plot line, and a stunning ending (that is actually a new beginning).

The trouble is, many Christians are simply living in the *world's* story and trying to make the Bible somehow relevant to that. That is, they shape all their assumptions and decisions along the same lines that the rest of the people around us in the world do—but try to add a dose of Bible gloss by "applying" Bible verses here and there. We sincerely try to apply the Bible to "my life"—which sounds fine but actually assumes that my life is the center of reality, to which the Bible has to be somehow fitted in an adjectival way. Or sometimes, worse, we use the Bible selectively to reinforce our own personal aspirations, social and political views, or delusions.

We have seriously lost the plot—the biblical plot. We have forgotten the story we are in.

The Bible tells the true story of the universe. It is like a great drama in seven acts.[1] The whole story can be captured in a simple diagram form:

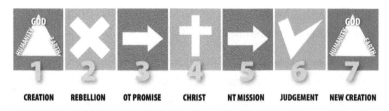

CREATION REBELLION OT PROMISE CHRIST NT MISSION JUDGEMENT NEW CREATION

Figure 7.1. The Seven Acts of Scripture

Act 1: Creation. God created the heavens and earth, and placed human beings, made in his own image, on the earth to rule and serve there, in a triangle of creational relationships between God, humanity, and the earth.

Act 2: Rebellion. We chose to disobey God's instructions and to choose for ourselves what we think is good and evil. We brought sin, death, and division into human life, and brokenness into creation itself.

Act 3: Old Testament promise. God promised that he would bring blessing and salvation where we had brought curse and death. Through Abraham he launched the people, Israel, through whom the good news of that blessing would ultimately embrace all nations on earth. The Old Testament story is constantly moving forward toward the fulfillment of that promise, with all the expectations and hopes that are generated within that part of the story.

Act 4: Christ. The central act of the whole Bible story is what we read in the gospel according to the first four books of the New Testament, about Jesus of Nazareth, Messiah and Lord: his incarnation, his life and teaching, his atoning death, his victorious resurrection, and his ascension to glory and cosmic government. This is the central act, the heartbeat and core of the biblical gospel.

Act 5: New Testament mission. The drama continues with the outpouring of the Holy Spirit and the launch of the mission of the church, comprising both believing Jews and Gentiles, to the ends of the earth. This part of the biblical story stretches from the day of Pentecost to the return of Christ.

Act 6: Final judgment. The good news is that evil will not have the last word and God will ultimately put all things right (which is what judgment means in the Bible) by dealing with and destroying all that is wrong and evil. Act 6 is the completion of God's answer to act 2 and of all that was accomplished in act 4. It will be the final rectification— the putting right of all that has been so disastrously wrong.

Act 7: New creation. The Bible drama ends with a dramatic new beginning! After putting all things right, God will make all things new and will come to dwell with redeemed humanity, in our resurrection bodies like Christ's, in God's reconciled creation. The creational triangle will be restored in glory: God dwelling with redeemed humanity in a reunited new heaven and earth. Then forever we will enjoy the presence of God with us ("Immanuel") and the absence of all that has spoiled, corrupted, and inflicted pain and suffering in the present fallen world.

These seven acts of the biblical drama can be mapped along the more familiar fourfold shape of the biblical worldview: creation (act 1), fall (act 2), redemption in history (acts 3–5), and future hope (acts 6–7).

Followers of Jesus are participants in this great biblical drama. We are called to live *in* this biblical story and *for* this story. That means that we should orient our lives in relation to what this story tells us about who we are and why we are here. It is this biblical story that gives us our identity and our mission as the people of God for the sake of God's mission. It is this story that tells us how we are to live in that part of the great drama where we find ourselves now.

The point is, *We are in the Bible!* I have found the diagram above incredibly helpful (it can be drawn on the back of an envelope or a restaurant napkin) in explaining what is meant by saying that we are called to play our part in God's story. By asking, "Where (in which act) would you place yourself in this great drama?" the answer is, fairly obviously,

"In act 5." The resurrection of Christ is a fact of past history. The return of Christ is an eagerly awaited event of the future. We live somewhere in between those two pivotal and climactic biblical moments, in act 5, engaged in the mission that the risen Christ mandated until he returns.

"What story are you living in?" is a question I often ask, especially among younger followers of Jesus. The right and challenging answer is that we are participants in act 5 of the Bible's great drama. We live there in the light of what God has already done and said in acts 1–4 (the past story of Israel; the teaching of the Law and Prophets; the worship and wisdom of Israel; the life, work, and teaching of Christ; and the teaching of the apostles). We live there also in the light of what God will do in the guaranteed future of acts 6 and 7 (the certainty of ultimate rectification in the final judgment and the guarantee of the new creation and all that will be true then, and all that and will *not* be true then). Our lives should be governed by this great, overarching story of the Bible. Our present should be shaped by the biblical past and the biblical future.[2] This is *our narrative*. This is who *we* are, as Christian believers, and what we are about in the world.

In other words, living as Bible people is not just a matter of applying the Bible to my life. Rather, it is the other way around. We should ask, "How can I apply my life, my little life in the here and now of this generation, into the great story of the Bible? How can I live in such a way as to fit into this story, to participate in what God is doing, and prepare for all he plans for the future? How can my life, my choices, my behavior, my thoughts and actions belong within this great story, with some measure of worthiness and consistency?"

We could take Daniel as our model. He lived and worked in Babylon but prayed every day with his windows open toward Jerusalem (Dan 6:10). I do not think that was mere nostalgia or daydreaming. Rather, Daniel served the king of Babylon, but his life was governed by the King who had placed his name on Jerusalem and by the standards and values that his God had invested in the story and Scriptures of his own people, Israel. Surrounded by the gods of Babylon and serving the government of Babylon, Daniel remained true to the God of Israel. We, too, have to live in Babylon, but we do not live for Babylon or by Babylon's story, or seduced by Babylon's gods. We live *in* the world but not by the world's story, but rather by the story of God—the full biblical revelation.

Returning to our main concern—resisting the idols and living a radically God-centered life—this requires that we soak ourselves in the Bible itself. It cannot be accidental that the rise of syncretism and cultural captivity to the gods of the people around us in Western Christianity goes along with an alarming decline in biblical literacy, even among so-called evangelical Christians. When God's people lose the knowledge of God's Word (or even lose interest in it altogether), then naturally they forget God's story—the story we are supposed to be in. Other gods fill the vacuum. Resisting idolatry requires a return to serious and systematic personal Bible reading and to lively, planned, and nourishing biblical preaching.

We must be gospel people: committed to the mission of God

Followers of Jesus are on a mission, as he was. He was sent, and so are we. "As the Father sent me into the world, so I send you into the world." Discipleship is, therefore, by definition missional. We are *all* included in the mandate of the Great Commission. "All authority in heaven and on earth has been given to me. Therefore go and make disciples of all nations, baptizing them in the name of the Father and of the Son and of the Holy Spirit, and teaching them to obey everything I have commanded you. And surely I am with you always, to the very end of the age" (Mt 28:18-20). This commission begins and ends with God; it begins with the affirmation of the lordship of Christ, and it ends with the promise of the presence of Christ—in both cases using God language. It all flows from the truth of the universal lordship of Christ over all creation. Jesus claims the Yahweh position—God of all creation. Mission itself is (or should be) radically God-centered. We do what we do because God is who God is and because God does what God does.

All our mission flows from the mission of God. That is an utterly crucial point to grasp.

Indeed, Christ's opening words in Matthew 28:18 strongly echo Deuteronomy 4:39. Moses has been addressing the Israelites about their God, in a chapter that resolutely seeks to turn Israel away from any and all kinds of false gods. "Acknowledge and take to heart this day that the LORD is God in heaven above and on the earth below. There is no other" (Deut 4:39). The Lord God of Israel is God of heaven and earth (that is, the whole creation). This is a truth about God that the Old Testament repeats all over the place, especially in the psalms. Jesus, standing on the Mount of Ascension, calmly takes that truth about the God whom all his followers know and worship and claims it for himself. Not surprisingly, Matthew records that when they met Jesus there, "they worshiped him" (though he also points out with frank honesty that some doubted). They now knew that as they met with the crucified and risen Christ they were in the presence of the living God, Yahweh, Creator of heaven and earth.

Whatever our mission may include, then, in all its breadth and comprehensiveness, it takes as its assurance and authority that Jesus is Lord of creation, that the earth belongs to him. He is the landlord, and we are his tenants. The earth is his property, and we are stewards of it, accountable to him for what we do on and with it.

So our mission is to the ends of the earth and until the end of the world—for all time and space on this planet. *All* disciples, all followers of Jesus, are mandated to obey this self-replicating instruction. We are, in short, on mission as soon as we submit our lives to Jesus Christ as Lord and Savior.

But what exactly is included in our mission?

Many proposals have been made over the years to define and describe the mission of the church. One that I find helpful (though it is far from the only one) is the so-called five marks of mission.[3] They can be summarized in a few words: *evangelism, teaching, compassion, justice,* and *stewardship of creation.* It is a remarkably comprehensive and holistic list, and each item can be shown to have deep roots in the whole Bible.

Furthermore, all five marks can be considered as ways in which we participate in the mission of God—that is, they are activities whereby *we* engage in what God himself does or wills to be done. When we do these things, God is actively participating with us and we with him, for these things are clearly identified in the Bible as passionate concerns of God.

Once again, we need to recall the challenge of radical God-centeredness, in our mission as in all else. So it is crucial that we put at the center of these five marks of mission the opening affirmation of the Great Commission—the lordship of Christ over all creation. That is what generates each of them and at the same time provides the integrating center that holds them all together.

All of those five dimensions of mission depend on the lordship of Christ. So here they are, linked together around the centrality of the gospel truth that Jesus is Lord. That, after all, is what the gospel of the kingdom means—that God's reign is inaugurated and embodied in Jesus himself, as Messiah and Lord. The good news is that God is king and God's kingship is exercised through Jesus of Nazareth in his earthly life, in his atoning death and resurrection, and in his sovereign reign at God's right hand as "ruler of the kings of the earth" (Rev 1:5).

- In evangelism, we proclaim the good news that Jesus Christ is Lord, King, and Savior. This emphasizes the centrality of the gospel in all authentic biblical mission.
- In teaching, we bring people into maturity of faith and discipleship, in submission to Christ as Lord.
- In compassion, we follow the example of the Lord Jesus, who "went around doing good" (Acts 10:38).
- In seeking justice, we remember that the Lord Jesus Christ is the judge of all the earth and that all justice ultimately flows from the throne of God, where he is seated.
- In properly fulfilling our vocation within creation, using and caring for all that God has entrusted to our rule as kings and priests, we are handling what belongs to the Lord Jesus Christ by right of creation and redemption.

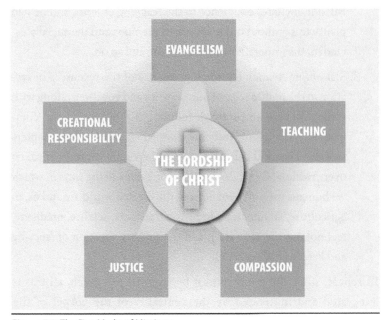

Figure 7.2. The Five Marks of Mission

We can simplify things still further by putting evangelism and teaching together and putting compassion and justice together. That then creates three major missional tasks, or three focal points for our missional engagement: church, society, and creation. Our mission, then, includes:

1. *Building the church* (through evangelism and teaching), bringing people to repentance, faith, and obedience as disciples of Jesus Christ. We should remember that a local church's program of preaching, teaching and discipling is as much a dimension of its mission, in fulfillment of the Great Commission ("teaching them to obey everything I commanded you"), as its explicitly evangelistic outreach or missionary sending.

2. *Serving society* (through compassion and justice), in response to Jesus sending us into the world to love and serve, to be salt and light, to do good works, and to "seek the prosperity" of the people around us (as Jeremiah told the Israelites in Babylon, Jer 29:7).

Mission includes obedience to the teaching of Jesus, and he had plenty to say about our response to the poor and the socially excluded, the imperative of compassion, and so on.

3. *Stewarding creation* (through godly use of the resources of creation in the multiplicity of human work and vocations, along with ecological care and action), fulfilling the very first great commission given to humanity in Genesis 1–2. In those two chapters we see a beautiful balance between the kingly vocation of ruling over creation (Gen 1:26-28; which includes all the ways in which we humans use and benefit from the created world around us, in agriculture, architecture, industry, transport, science, medicine, technology, the arts, etc.), and the priestly vocation of "serving and keeping" (Gen 2:15).

To repeat, since the point cannot be stressed too much, all this is integrated and motivated by the centrality of the gospel of the kingdom of God in the lordship of Jesus Christ. Everything flows from that. We build the church because Jesus is Lord of the church.

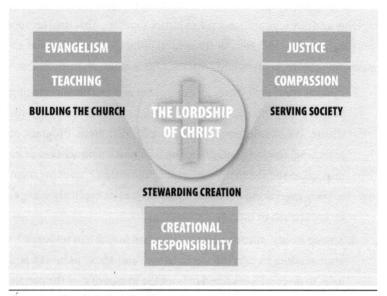

Figure 7.3. Church, Society, Creation

We serve society because Jesus (and not Caesar) is Lord of every nation, government, and culture (whether acknowledged as such or not). We manage creation with godly use and care, because Jesus is Lord of heaven *and earth*—"the earth is the LORD's, and everything in it" (Ps 24:1). Every dimension of our mission flows from the lordship of Christ, and from the will and mission of God that the whole world and all creation will come to recognize that fact, and in doing so will come to know, love, praise, and worship our Creator and Redeemer.

This triple scope of mission is fully biblical. The Cape Town Commitment recognizes that all three need to be held together in a truly holistic and integrated understanding of mission.

> Integral mission means discerning, proclaiming, and living out, the biblical truth that the gospel is God's good news, through the cross and resurrection of Jesus Christ, for individual persons, *and* for society, *and* for creation. All three are broken and suffering because of sin; all three are included in the redeeming love and mission of God; all three must be part of the comprehensive mission of God's people.[4]

There is no space to expound all of these areas of mission further here.[5] But their comprehensiveness can function as a useful tool for churches to do a mission audit. The church to which I belong, All Souls Church, Langham Place, London, uses all five marks of mission as a template for the whole range of its mission service and support, at home and abroad. We seek to support, fund, and pray for missional engagement and action in all five areas, while being careful to build everything on the foundation of, and test everything by the criterion of, the centrality of the gospel of the kingdom of God embodied in the lordship of Christ over the whole of life.

The point I want to stress in the context of our topic here, however, is this. Even in the midst of political change and chaos, even in turbulent times, even when the gods and idols of our cultures are rampant and apparently triumphant, even when we discern the outworking of God's judgment in our own nations—*nevertheless, our mission goes on.*

When Jeremiah wrote his letter to the first batch of exiles of Judah in Babylon in 597 BC (soon to be followed by the second much larger captivity after the destruction of Jerusalem ten years later), those people were enduring the most traumatic experience of the whole history of Israel to that point. It seemed that evil had triumphed and the pagan gods and idols had won. Nebuchadnezzar had not only defeated King Zedekiah; the gods of Babylon had also defeated Yahweh—or so it seemed. Why, even his temple had been ransacked, desecrated, and burned to the ground! What sort of god could not save his own temple (the question Isaiah asked about the gods of Babylon and their statues)?

But Jeremiah gave them a different perspective: Yahweh God of Israel was still in control. It was Yahweh (not merely Nebuchadnezzar) who had sent them into exile. Even though the exile was indeed the outworking of God's judgment on Israel, and even though Babylon itself stood in the blast path of God's judgment yet to come (just skim through Jer 50–51)—*nevertheless*, in precisely such terrifying times, God gave also his people a fresh mission, which must have seemed outrageously surprising in the circumstances: "Also, seek the peace and prosperity of the city to which I have carried you into exile. Pray to the LORD for it, because if it prospers, you too will prosper" (Jer 29:7). They were still the people of Abraham, still the people created to be a blessing to the nations—including enemy nations. So let them settle down in Babylon and, until God's time would come for that whole civilization, let them seek the good of the people around them and pray for them. This is very close to "Love your enemies" in Old Testament dress. Even in exile under judgment, God's people had a mission—the original mission for which God had called Abraham centuries earlier. I rather like to think that Daniel and his three friends were among the exiles who heard Jeremiah's letter read out—and did exactly what it said. How else can we explain Daniel's apparent affection and goodwill toward Nebuchadnezzar in Daniel 4, other than by assuming Daniel was praying for his pagan boss in the midst of his thrice-daily prayers? It is hard to go on hating someone you are praying for every day.

Likewise we as Christians, even in the midst of a collapsing culture and civilization in which the marks of God's judgment are very evident, are not called to abandon ship but to go on fulfilling our mission, serving the purpose for which God created us as his people. To work and serve and seek the welfare of the community around us; to bear witness to the living God and the salvation he offers through Christ, even when it is costly; and to pray for the world and its rulers, even when they mock and deny the very God we are praying to.

Christ gave his Great Commission (that phrase was not his, of course, but ours) to a tiny group of his followers in the midst of the overwhelming power and hostility of both religious and secular authorities. He had also given them plenty of warning about the reality and the signs of God's judgment to come (and more was to follow when he gave his revelation to John). Yet they went out into the world that proclaimed "Caesar is Lord!" and countered that claim with the bold and crazy (to most ears) affirmation, "*Jesus* is Lord!"

"Yes!" they declared, "Jesus, the crucified Messiah of Israel (!), is Lord! And we come to bring that fact to you as good news, a fact corroborated by his eyewitnessed resurrection and the manifest power of his Holy Spirit. And on the basis of that good news we call you to repent, to put your faith in Jesus, and to submit to him in obedient discipleship. Then you will receive God's forgiveness of your sins, and you will become citizens of God's kingdom, members of God's family; indeed, you will actually become part of a whole new way of being human. You will join a very different story with a much better destiny—life eternal in God's new creation."

Ours is still the same missional task, in a world not greatly different from theirs.

Ours, too, is the same calling: to live as citizens of the kingdom of God that Jesus came proclaiming. The call to discipleship was fundamentally a challenge to accept and submit to the reign of God and to shape the whole of life accordingly. That was the message of John the Baptist, followed by Jesus. It is the same call and challenge that faces us today.

We must be kingdom people: submitting to the reign of God

We should not imagine that Jesus *invented* the idea of the kingdom of God. It was already a thoroughly familiar concept to all his fellow Jews, nourished by the worship of Israel and longing for the fulfillment of prophetic visions. "The Lord reigns!" sang the psalmists—both as a statement of present reality (Yahweh truly is sovereign over all creation) and as an affirmation of future hope. For when Yahweh's reign will be fully acknowledged by all peoples, then will come the time of eschatological righteousness and justice, peace and harmony. Then all creation will rejoice before the Lord when he comes to judge the earth (which means, to put all things right; see Ps 96:10-13).

> So the kingship of God in Israel had very *practical, earthy effects*. It was not just a theological item of belief. It was the authority of God as king, which lay behind the specific details of Israel's law. . . . There was, therefore, a powerfully *ethical* thrust to the acknowledgment of Yahweh's kingship. His reign was one of *righteousness and justice,* earthed in the real world of social, economic and political relationships. And this is what we find in some of the Psalms which celebrate it . . . [e.g. Ps 97:2; 99:4; 145:8-9; 146:7-10]. . . .
>
> The kingdom of God, then, meant the reign of *Yahweh,* and where Yahweh is king, justice and compassion must reign too. . . .
>
> So when Jesus came proclaiming the kingdom of God, he was not talking about a faraway place or an ideal or an attitude. It was not just pie in the sky or joy in the heart. The reality of God's rule

cannot be spiritualized into heaven (now or later) or privatized into individuals. Of course, it does have spiritual and personal dimensions, which are fundamental also. We are called to submit to God's reign in our individual lives. But the term itself speaks of the aligning of human life on earth, in all its dimensions, with the will of the divine government of God. To pray "may your kingdom come," is to pray, "may your will be done on earth as in heaven." The one must produce the other.[6]

So when Jesus announced the arrival of God's reign, the shock to his contemporaries was not in the term itself but in both his insistence that it was *here and present now among them* and in the fact that it had invaded but not yet eliminated the kingdoms of this world, the old order of sin, oppression, poverty, violence, suffering, and death. So his parables likened it to things that start small but, in hidden and inexplicable ways, grow irresistibly larger; to something hidden but infinitely precious and worth selling all you have to obtain; to a process that will sift and divide humanity until a final reckoning by God himself; to something that you have to enter not by power and wealth and achievement but by childlike humility and servanthood. The kingdom of God would turn the world (and the kingdoms of this world) radically upside down—or, rather, the right way up.

> But the point was, the reign of God had definitely arrived. It was inaugurated. It was present and at work right there in the midst of the people, said Jesus. It gave them an opportunity they must not miss. And it made demands they could not evade—demands which they already knew about from the riches of their Scriptures and all the moral depths of Old Testament faith. . . .
>
> In its major features the kingdom of God already had its *essential ethical* content from the Old Testament. The kingdom of God was already filled with the whole range of ethical values, priorities and demands [recorded] in the law and the prophets. If Yahweh God has come to reign, then the Scriptures had

already shown clearly what that would mean for God's people and for the world.

There was no ambiguity at all about what was required of the people of God under his kingship. No ambiguity about what it would mean for the world when God would establish his rule. The dynamic power of the message of Jesus lay not so much in *what* the kingdom of God meant as in *the fact that it had arrived.* The gospel that Jesus preached was good news of a present reality. Good news of the kingdom of God. Good news, at least, for those who were prepared to receive it in repentant hearts and a radical new agenda for living.[7]

So then, those whom Jesus first called to be his followers knew both the challenge and the potential cost of living as citizens of the kingdom of God in a political world that boasted the kingdom of Caesar and Rome, and in a religious world that borrowed at least some of its coercive power from that dominant kingdom.

For them, living under the reign of God as taught by their master, Jesus, meant rejecting several opposing options, to which many of their contemporaries succumbed.

On the one hand, it meant rejecting collusion with the political power and wealth of Rome (what we might call the right-wing option). That was the choice the Sadducees had made, who were among the most insistent that Jesus of Nazareth posed a threat to their surrendered accommodation with Rome. Later, of course, Paul and Peter told followers of Jesus who had no option but to live within the Roman Empire that they should be good citizens, pay their taxes, and honor the emperor. That remains a Christian ethical duty, in relation to human governments. But when followers of Jesus are tempted, like the Sadducees, to praise, justify, and collude with corrupt and greedy political regimes for their own religious protection and privileges, to such an extent that they jettison the values of the kingdom of God and the teachings of his Christ, then the warning lights of insidious idolatry begin to flash.

On the other hand, the kingdom of God for disciples of Jesus meant rejecting other radical alternatives to collusion with Rome (which we might call the left-wing options). These might be religious (such as the Essenes, who withdrew into the wilderness to pursue a separatist kind of eschatological purity) or revolutionary (such as the Zealots, who waged violent guerrilla warfare against occupying Roman forces on behalf of the oppressed poor). Collusion, withdrawal, violence—these are not options Jesus commends to his own followers, then or now.

Rather, they were called to practice the values of *God's* kingdom, as taught and modeled by Jesus himself, even while they necessarily had to live in Caesar's kingdom. They were to be "in the world but not of it" (see 1 Jn 2:15). Such practices included the things Jesus himself did or told them to do—breaking down social barriers, practicing costly for-giveness and table fellowship with those whom society despised, can-celing debts, turning the other cheek, offering generosity to the poor and the outsider, loving even the enemy, welcoming the outcast. These were radical and subversive of the established order, the social bound-aries, and the religious codes of their day, both Jewish and Roman. Dis-ciples of Christ were called to a very different way of living and relating, shaped by Jesus and his kingdom, not Herod's or Caesar's.[8]

What does it mean for us? We need to recognize clearly the difference between the kingdom of God as taught and modeled by Jesus (including the way of suffering and death) and the Christendom way of thinking. The era known historically as Christendom began with the "conversion" of the Emperor Constantine and his Edict of Milan (AD 313), making Christianity a legal religion in the Roman Empire. Eventually, Christians began to take over some of the trappings, status symbols, and culture of the empire itself. It is remarkable how quickly Christianity morphed from being a persecuted community for some three centuries into a persecuting religiopolitical power throughout Europe for the next thirteen or so. An unholy alliance emerged, on the one hand, between "the Christian religion" and massive ecclesiastical wealth and power (very far distant from the teaching and example of Christ and his apostles) and, on the other hand, between religious and secular powers and authorities—prelates and princes. It seemed natural, perhaps even providential, that the power of the state should promote and protect the interests of Christianity, while it might be hoped that Christianity would sanctify the workings of the state. Unfortunately, the price Christianity paid for its protection was its own corruption and complicity in the greed, ambition, immorality, endless conflicts, and endemic violence of all-too-fallen and sinful human power structures, and those who used them for their own enrichment. In gaining the world (or at least a continent), we lost our own soul.[9]

When we declare that Jesus is Lord and not Caesar, we are acknowledging that we are called to follow the Jesus of the cross, not the Jesus of Constantine.

European Christendom ended with the exhaustion of religious wars and the secularizing acids of the Enlightenment. But Christendom ways of thinking are still around. There is still a curious imagination, flying in the face of the Bible's insistence that there is only one Savior and Lord on the throne of the universe, that the best way for Christians to save the world would be for Christians to rule the world, or at least, that part of the world we might have some realistic hope of ruling over by having Christians in the seats of government. There is still a curious expectation, flying in the face of all that the Old Testament teaches us about the tendency of all political power to go rogue and produce a downward spiral of combined idolatry and injustice, that having a Christian as president or prime minister will somehow purge and rectify the whole systemic fallenness of political structures whose ideals have been corroded by centuries of self-interest, tribal allegiance, and privilege.[10]

This is not to say that Christians should stay out of the political arena. The way of complete withdrawal is not a valid biblical option. As we shall see in the next chapter, there is a valid and honorable vocation for Christians in the political sphere—engaged but distinctive, as salt and light. I give thanks to God for many Christian members of Parliament in the United Kingdom. What I am questioning is not Christian *involvement* in politics but the idea that Christians should seek *supremacy* in the political arena, in the belief that such legislative, judicial, or coercive power would enable them to advance the gospel or build the kingdom of God by political means—especially if, in order to gain such power, we sacrifice our integrity to whatever false gods happen to dominate the political arena of the day.

This Christendom mentality imagines that the kingdom of God can be advanced by getting "our man in the White House"—the precise words that a dear American friend said to me when I landed in the United States a few days after a previous presidential election. "He holds a prayer meeting in the Oval Office!" she went on, with obvious delight. I could not help but recall the prophet Amos (though I was too polite to do so out loud). Perhaps King Jeroboam II was holding prayer meetings in his palace too. Certainly religious worship was thriving all over the country. But, said Amos, God was not interested in religious profession by the government or anybody else but in public morality. God's eyes were not on the temple or palace but on what was happening in wider society. According to Amos, God's righteous eyes saw the corruption in the courts under the power of wealth and patronage, the gross social inequality, the offensive extravagances of the rich, the dehumanizing evil of crushing debt and poverty, the suffering of the poor and dispossessed, the manipulation of economic systems for personal gain, the war on truth and integrity. In today's world, has God shifted his gaze? What matters to God, Amos would say, is not what a president says in his prayers but what his government does in practice and whether that aligns in any degree at all with the standards of justice and compassion that God's Word makes very clear are the responsibilities of those entrusted with political power.

I could also illustrate the point, for the sake of fair balance, by noting a similar dissonance in the United Kingdom. A recent former prime minister was well known to be the daughter of a pastor and faithful in regular attendance at the local Anglican church. But in her previous post as home secretary, she instituted a policy of creating a "hostile environment" (her own words) toward illegal immigrants, in the ferment of anti-immigrant popular opinion that so infected (indeed, was a major trigger for) the Brexit referendum and its outcome. Unfortunately, the policy became a hostile net that caught up many hundreds of people, mainly from the Caribbean, who had come to the United Kingdom perfectly legally as children with their parents, at the invitation of the British government to address the country's severe labor shortage in the years after the Second World War.[11] Suddenly, having lived and worked in the United Kingdom all their lives, they were deemed illegal unless they could provide multiple forms of documentary evidence proving otherwise. As home secretary, she was responsible for a departmental policy that led to many from this community being wrongfully detained, denied legal rights, denied their entitlement to hospital treatment for serious illness, losing their jobs and homes, falling into destitution, and in some cases being wrongfully deported. Many of these were elderly and vulnerable people, and their suffering was (and in many cases remains) immense and scandalous—and entirely caused by the hostile power of a state that had initially welcomed them when it needed their labor. So again, it has to be asked, In the light of the biblical standards of the kingdom of God, what value can be accorded to a politician's Christian profession and churchgoing if their politics in actual practice are inflicting humiliating suffering on those whose lives were already blighted by the historic racism of British culture?

What about us who are simply citizens, most of us not destined for political office, but all of us (in democratic countries at least) vested with the political power of our votes?

We need to reexamine our loyalties and ask whether we have submitted our political views, choices, and support to the criteria of God's kingdom as revealed in the Old Testament and the teaching of Jesus and the apostles, or whether we are giving colluding praise and approval to corrupt and immoral political power in the hope that it might somehow benefit the cause of Christ.

Now, that is not by any means a simple and straightforward thing to do, of course. Whether in a representative parliamentary system (such as the United Kingdom), or a constitutional presidential system (such as the United States), our choice is never merely between one *person* and another. We must also choose between one *party* and another, which brings whole packages of policies, positions, and objectives onto the table for us to evaluate. Speaking at least from the British point of view (where our politics is much less polarized between two binary parties than in the United States), it is rare if ever that a Christian voter will agree with every policy or stance of any single political party. So a choice has to be made on the basis of evaluating the overall thrust or balance of a particular party and political program, as to whether, allowing for those aspects one inevitably disagrees with, there is at least some partial alignment or compatibility with major biblical values in the social realm. That further requires, of course, that we have done some thinking about *what the Bible's own ethical priorities actually are*, rather than assuming that the moral issues that we are most passionate about are entirely identical to those that the Bible, or Jesus, would prioritize. It is too easy for our moral hot spots to hide moral blind spots.

For example, there is no doubt that the Bible condemns the many sinful forms in which our fallen and disordered human sexuality manifests itself. Nor can there be any doubt that the confused and disordered state of sexual attitudes and behavior in late modern Western societies is displeasing to God, contrary to the Bible, and massively destructive of human stability and well-being, especially for children. There are, unquestionably, major moral issues to be faced here in the social, ecclesial, and political realms.

But there is equally no doubt, for it is statistically very clear, that the Bible has far, far more to say in condemnation of social and economic evils than about the evils of sexual misconduct. The offensive misery of crippling debt, poverty, and dispossession; the exploitation of workers; ill treatment of the homeless, familyless, landless, and disabled; the vulnerability of widows, orphans, and foreigners—all of these loom large and often in the Law, the Prophets, and the wisdom literature.[12] Many psalms rail against those in positions of wealth and power who perpetuate such evils, crying out to God on the assumption (based on their familiarity with the character and priorities of God revealed in the Torah), that *God himself must care about such things at least as much as the psalmist does.*

But do *we* care? That is, do we care at the point when we make a political decision on how our votes will be cast? Or have we somehow removed the issue of poverty and the suffering it causes from our category of moral issues in the political realm—in spite of the fact that it would be among the highest moral priorities in the Bible's own evaluation of political responsibility? We may feel it our duty to vote for a person who, we believe, will uphold or restore certain legal protections or civil advantages for Christians and churches and institutions, in the face of increasing societal and political intolerance toward religious faith in general and overt Christian faith in particular. For it is true that secular antipathy and intolerance toward any public expression of Christian faith is increasing in Western countries, along with condemnation of choices and actions based on Christian moral conscience and sometimes quite brutal expulsion from the workplace.

However, if the person or party that we hope will protect our Christian rights also proposes (or already has a historical record of pursuing) economic and fiscal policies that will favor the already rich and increase the multiple disadvantages of the already poor, does that not at least give us pause for biblical reflection on our political priorities? What might Jesus say or think about the relative importance of protecting our own rights and civic status as Christians as over against caring for the poorest in society? Since when, in any case, did our calling and mission to live as Christians and to bear witness to the truth of the gospel by words and deeds that faithfully live out our loyalty to Jesus Christ *depend on* favorable state authorities and conducive legal and political circumstances? That was certainly not the way it was for the New Testament churches under the Roman Empire, and it certainly *is* not the case for the vast majority of the world's Christians today.

So, as we ponder the moral and theological challenge of our electoral choices, we may end up in the well-known ethical dilemma of having to choose the lesser of two evils. Christian voters in recent elections in both the United States and the United Kingdom have been faced with having to choose between candidates who in multiple ways were (are) deeply flawed—not just in the way that any candidate for political office is a fallen sinner like the rest of us, but on an extreme scale of habitual untruthfulness, sexual promiscuity, and arrogant narcissism, or with taints of political and social attitudes that we simply cannot condone as biblically acceptable. What then?

With a great deal of thought and prayer, and doing our best not simply to act out of tribal loyalty to the party we always supported, we have to look squarely at those "two evils" and come to some decision as to which is, in the light of the biblical standards of the kingdom of God, likely to be the lesser one. We may choose to vote not for what or whom we consider good but for what or whom we consider, on balance, less bad. That can be a painful and reluctant choice. But having made it, we may feel able to justify it to our conscience and before the Lord.

What seems to me much less able to be justified is the temptation then, if the less bad alternative succeeds and enters the long historical roll call of state authorities who have been in some sense given temporary power under the sovereign governance of God, to shower them with accolades of praise and approval that overlook or whitewash their moral depravity by biblical standards. God may use evil persons to accomplish his sovereign purposes in history—the Bible has plenty of examples of that. That neither exonerates their evil nor gives us liberty to extol them.

However, even if we follow the prophets and rightly condemn rather than praise immoral rulers (praising and pleasing wicked rulers was a classic mark of the *false* prophets), we must at the same time avoid the hypocrisy of living lives that are indistinguishable from the culture around us. Living in and for the kingdom of God must mean living a life that is different from the kingdoms of this world.

CHAPTER EIGHT

FOLLOWING JESUS IN TURBULENT TIMES

T HE CALL TO HOLINESS remains as stark and challenging for us today as it was for Old Testament Israel and the first Christian believers (e.g., 1 Pet). That inevitably means that we must be *different*. Those who follow Jesus must be as distinctive as he was.

We must be distinctive people: shining the light of God

We live in a political era defined now not only by change (it always was) but by *lies* (so-called posttruth culture). Demonstrable falsehoods, exaggerations, unsubstantiated boasts, inconsistent claims made one day and retracted the next—such have become the tragically new normal from the White House. The Brexit referendum campaign in the United Kingdom, and the whole political process that followed it, was marked by public mendacity on an industrial scale, magnified through the unaccountable power of social media. There were exaggerated and unfulfillable promises based on statistics that were demonstrably false but never retracted even when proven to be so. There was unrelenting demonizing and blaming of the weak and poor for social problems of which they were the victims, not the cause. There was blatant racism and xenophobic hatred, stoked by politicians and the tabloid press. All this against a wider background of corruption, nepotism, self-enrichment, and darkness in high places. All of these things, surely, would be included among the kind of spiritual powers of evil that Paul warns us about in Ephesians 6.

In such a world, one that is much the same as it was in the Roman Empire of New Testament days, Jesus calls his followers to be salt and light, his powerful combination of metaphors in the Sermon on the Mount (Mt 5:13-16). Both light and salt have a transforming impact on their surroundings. Light dispels darkness. Salt stems putrefaction. Jesus was challenging his followers to a have comparable dynamic impact on their surroundings through penetrating engagement combined with radical distinctiveness.

"You are the light of the world," says Jesus (Mt 5:14). What on earth did he mean by such a sweeping statement? Did he mean that his disciples would be preachers of the truth of the gospel that would bring light to people in the darkness of ignorance and sin? Yes, of course he would have included that in the overall task of the apostolic mission, as Paul explains using the same metaphor in 2 Corinthians 4:4-6. But look again at what Jesus actually stresses when he explains what he means by light. "Let your light shine before others, that they may see *your good deeds* and glorify your Father in heaven" (Mt 5:16, emphasis added). When Jesus talks about light he is speaking of *lives* that are attractive by being filled with goodness, mercy, love, compassion, and justice—and whatever else might constitute good deeds.[1]

As he regularly did, Jesus is drawing here on a strong Old Testament tradition. God had called Israel to be a light to the nations, and that included the quality of their lives as a society. Light as a metaphor had a strongly ethical and social meaning. Isaiah, for example, combines light and righteousness. Light shines from people committed to compassion and justice. Isaiah goes on to say that such light, because it reflects the light of God's own presence and glory among his people, will draw the nations. God's light, shining in God's people who are themselves transformed by it, is missionally attractive (Is 60:1-3). It will bring people to glorify the living God. Is that not exactly what Jesus says?

Is not this the kind of fasting I have chosen:
to loose the chains of injustice
    and untie the cords of the yoke,
to set the oppressed free
    and break every yoke?
Is it not to share your food with the hungry
    and to provide the poor wanderer with shelter—
when you see the naked, to clothe them,
    and not to turn away from your own flesh and blood?
Then *your light* will break forth like the dawn,
    and your healing will quickly appear;
then *your righteousness* will go before you. . . .

And if you spend yourselves in behalf of the hungry
    and satisfy the needs of the oppressed,
then *your light* will rise in the darkness,
    and your night will become like the noonday. (Is 58:6-8, 10
        emphasis added)

So then, in the Old Testament God commanded Israel to be a people committed to practical, down-to-earth exercise of compassion and justice, in ways that would reflect and embody God's own commitment to those things. Jesus both endorsed that mandate for his disciples (and indeed radically deepened it) and in the Great Commission commanded them to pass it on to the new disciples they would make ("teaching them to obey everything I have commanded you," Mt 28:20). Both in their life as a community of disciples and in their mission of making disciples, they must reflect the character of the God who cares for the poor and needy, who defends the cause of the widow and orphan. They did, as the book of Acts and Paul's letters and actions make clear.

Both metaphors, salt and light, speak of contrast and distinctiveness. As mentioned above, salt was primarily used to stem putrefaction in meat or fish, while little oil lamps were used to give light in the darkness of a room or street. Jesus' statement makes two assumptions, as we apply the sharp point of his metaphors: (1) that the world around us is both corrupt and dark, and (2) that followers of Jesus do have the power to make a difference to the world around them—just as salt and light do in the environments where they are activated.

If we go on to draw out the implications of Jesus' metaphors, we can say that, as Christians, we must therefore both (1) *penetrate* society (not withdraw from it) by fully engaging in all aspects of the public arena, including the workplace and the political sphere, and also (2) retain our *distinctiveness* within society. Penetrating distinctiveness is the Christian calling in the world, as salt and light. We are, as Jesus said, *in* the world, but we are not to be *of* the world—that is, the world does not own us; we belong to only one Master; we are different.[2]

John Stott liked to make this point very powerfully as follows:[3]

- If meat goes rotten when it is left out in the open, there is no point blaming the meat. That is what happens in its natural state—bacterial putrefaction sets in. The question to ask is, Where was the salt?
- If a room goes dark in the evening, there is no point blaming the room. That is what happens when the sun goes down. The question to ask is, Where is the lamp?
- If society goes rotten, corrupt, and evil, there is no point merely blaming society. That is what happens in a world full of fallen sinners left to themselves. The question to ask is, Where are the Christians?

But if there is no real difference . . . that is, if Christians are in most practical ways no different from the people and the culture around them, then we become nothing less than part of the problem itself— contributing to the division and degeneration of society. When Christians are just as bad as the rest in the eyes of the world ("And she calls herself a Christian!"), they raise severe and justified questions about the nature of our Christian faith.

The church faces massive problems of credibility and authenticity when it is rocked by scandals of sexual abuse, or pilloried for the obscene wealth of some of its celebrity preachers, or when even the word *evangelical* is grievingly disowned by many of our Christian sisters and brothers around the world because of the toxic political associations it has acquired in the United States.

Here is how the Cape Town Commitment, from the Third Lausanne Congress on World Evangelization in October 2010, expresses this challenge. Notice, in relation to our theme in this book, that it discerns the root problem of idolatry:

> The people of God either walk in the way of the Lord, or walk in the ways of other gods. The Bible shows that God's greatest problem is not just with the nations of the world, but with the people he has created and called to be the means of blessing the nations. And the biggest obstacle to fulfilling that mission is idolatry among God's own people. For if we are called to bring the nations to worship the only true and living God, we fail miserably if we ourselves are running after the false gods of the people around us.
>
> When there is no distinction in conduct between Christians and non-Christians—for example in the practice of corruption and greed, or sexual promiscuity, or rate of divorce, or relapse to pre-Christian religious practice, or attitudes towards people of other races, or consumerist lifestyles, or social prejudice—then the world is right to wonder if our Christianity makes any difference at all. Our message carries no authenticity to a watching world.
>
> a) We challenge one another, as God's people in every culture, to face up to the extent to which, consciously or unconsciously, we are caught up in the idolatries of our surrounding culture. We pray for prophetic discernment to identify and expose such false gods and their presence within the Church itself, and for the courage to repent and renounce them in the name and authority of Jesus as Lord.
>
> b) Since there is no biblical mission without biblical living, we urgently re-commit ourselves, and challenge all those who profess the name of Christ, to live in radical distinctiveness from the ways of the world, to "put on the new humanity, created to be like God in true righteousness and holiness."[4]

We must be praying people: appealing to the throne of God

Followers of Jesus must be people of prayer, as he was—so much so that his first followers asked him to teach them to pray *as he did* (they already were a praying people, from the habits of home and synagogue).

So he taught them the Lord's Prayer, which we blithely repeat with little thought about its challenging political significance.[5]

We begin, "Our Father in heaven." In those few words we immediately acknowledge that there is a higher throne—the God of Heaven, as Daniel called him, the One who is the "ruler of the kings of the earth" (Rev 1:5). Prayer is a political act, for it appeals to the Authority that is higher than the state's, whether emperor, or king, or president, or prime minister, or parliament, or supreme court. When you pray the opening words of the Lord's Prayer, you are effectively saying to *all* of those human authorities, "There is Someone above all of you." That is an act of political perspective. It puts all human authority in its proper relative position—subject to the governing authority of God in heaven.

Then we continue, "Your kingdom come, your will be done, on earth as in heaven"—that is an astonishing prayer! We are asking that the *rule* of God and the *will* of God should operate on earth—not just up in heaven, and not just at some point in the indefinite future. Do we understand it? Do we mean it? If we mean it, do we act in relation to that prayer, in connection with our political opinions, options, and decisions, as citizens and voters? Serious praying of the Lord's Prayer must include doing at least some of the hard thinking and decision making in the political realm that we were discussing very briefly in the section above on what it means to live as citizens of the kingdom of God.

It ought to mean, for example, that we search the Scriptures to see what God's *kingdom* actually means and demands in the Bible (and what we might expect if it were to come as we pray). Likewise, we would try to discern from multiple biblical texts that address social, economic, and political contexts what God's *will* is in those realms, according to the

Bible (and what it might mean if it were to be done as we pray). The point I am making is that in order to pray that prayer of Jesus intelligently and with integrity, we need to know our Bibles well enough (as he and his first disciples did) to understand what the *kingdom of God* and *the will* of God mean in relation to social, economic, and political life, and all the diverse realities of work and employment, the marketplace, business, the law courts, government, learning, the family, agriculture, health, creation itself, and so on. The Bible has plenty to say on all of those areas of life, and the Torah and the Prophets made it very clear what God's will in them is. Then, when we have done our biblical homework, we should *pray* for those values—the values of God's kingdom and God's will to be advocated and striven for on earth, in our own nation and neighborhood. Does that form any part of our desire or intentions when we repeat the words "Your kingdom come, your will be done, on earth as it is in heaven"?

If not, what is the point of the prayer?

What is the point of praying for God's reign to come and God's will to be done *on earth as in heaven*, if we do not even bother to think about what that means according the Scriptures God has given us, let alone act on what we discover?

Prayer in the political realm is actually commanded by Paul. "I urge, then, first of all, that petitions, prayers, intercession and thanksgiving be made for all people—for kings and all those in authority" (1 Tim 2:1-2). Paul commands all kinds of prayer for all kinds of rulers. Paul did not mean *Christian* kings and emperors—there were none! He meant prayer for the pagan Roman rulers of his world.

I have been in many, many church services all over the world, and I reckon this must be one of the most disobeyed instructions Paul ever issued. We get prayers for our needs, prayers for blessings, prayers for healing, prayers for missionaries (occasionally), prayers for world peace, and so on—but almost never any specific prayer in relation to whatever governing authorities are in power in any given country. (Anglican and Episcopal churches, usually, are an exception to this; prayers for governing authorities are built into the liturgy—provided it is used, of course.)

But what kind of prayer should we pray for the governing authorities? Just "God bless them"? "God give them wisdom"? Bland prayers that lack any precision or discernment? Prayers that could be prayed at any generic time, without real cutting relevance to contemporary political issues?

I was recently struck by the first ten psalms. Among them we find urgent, passionate, desperate prayer to God in relation to the political realm and its many evils. The psalmists pray that God would *put down* the wicked in power and *raise up* and vindicate the oppressed. Those prayers speak of nations and peoples and rulers and judges and hold them up to God's inspection. They assert that, if the Lord truly is king, then ultimately he *must* act in line with his own justice and put down the wicked from their high place and defend the cause of the oppressed (as Mary prayed in the Magnificat). Those biblical prayers do not hesitate to hurl real, raw, rank reality before God and ask him to *do something.* They are, in other words, deeply and desperately and unapologetically *political* prayers.

When did you last hear one of them used in a church service?

What would be the effect of praying Psalm 10 in the context of public worship, in full awareness of the culture of idolatry, wickedness, lies, greed, violence, and injustice that surrounds us, as it did the biblical psalmist? Reading it out loud as a prayer even by oneself, as I have done quite often, is a sobering exercise.

> Why, Lord, do you stand far off?
>   Why do you hide yourself in times of trouble?
>
> In his arrogance the wicked man hunts down the weak,
>   who are caught in the schemes he devises.
> He boasts about the cravings of his heart;
>   he blesses the greedy and reviles the Lord.
> In his pride the wicked man does not seek him;
>   in all his thoughts there is no room for God.
> His ways are always prosperous;
>   your laws are rejected by him;

he sneers at all his enemies.
He says to himself, "Nothing will ever shake me."
He swears, "No one will ever do me harm."

His mouth is full of lies and threats;
trouble and evil are under his tongue. . . .

Arise, LORD! Lift up your hand, O God.
Do not forget the helpless.
Why does the wicked man revile God?
Why does he say to himself,
"He won't call me to account"?
But you, God, see the trouble of the afflicted;
you consider their grief and take it in hand.
The victims commit themselves to you;
you are the helper of the fatherless.
Break the arm of the wicked man;
call the evildoer to account for his wickedness
that would not otherwise be found out. . . .

You, LORD, hear the desire of the afflicted;
you encourage them, and you listen to their cry,
defending the fatherless and the oppressed,
so that mere earthly mortals
will never again strike terror. (Ps 10:1-7, 12-15, 17-18)

Do we have the courage to pray like that? For surely, and very obviously, the things the psalmist protests about are still with us today, including the boasting of the wicked, and the powerless grief and suffering of their victims. These are prayers in the political realm that God has actually given us in Scripture, presumably intending that we should learn from them and use them appropriately. But instead, we tend to confine ourselves to psalms that provide us with personal comfort or affirm our faith or express our gratitude. Lament, protest, anger at duplicity and violence, longing for justice—these are noticeably present in biblical psalms *and noticeably absent in Christian prayer.*

I see no contradiction in both praying *for* our rulers and yet also praying *against* them.

I pray for them, in obedience to Paul's instructions, fully aware that they are human beings, sinners like myself in need of God's love and mercy. I pray that, insofar as they are persons of reasonable integrity and goodwill, God will give them wisdom and success in policies, legislation, and actions that are genuinely for the good of society. But I also pray *against* them when they pursue objectives and take actions that are manifestly out of line with what the Bible teaches as God's standards, values, and priorities for human well-being, or when their words and actions are clearly driven more by personal arrogance and ruthless ambition, or party advantage, than by truth, justice, and the common good.

When wickedness, lies, and corruption thrive, while the poor and marginalized sink into ever more debilitating destitution, should we not protest *to God*, personally, publicly, and often, that such things are scandalous, destructive, and evil, and pray *against* those who perpetuate them, including those who, from positions of political power and authority, collude with such wrongs or do little to put them right? I think the psalmists would probably say, "Go ahead. We did."

It will not do simply to appeal to Romans 13 and argue that since political authorities are appointed by God we must simply approve of all they do, or at least acquiesce therein and stay silent. That was not Isaiah's stance in relation to the government of his own day that was promulgating laws that embedded injustice by statute—a phenomenon that continues all over the world today, making his words as pointedly relevant as ever.

> Woe to those who make unjust laws,
>   to those who issue oppressive decrees,
> to deprive the poor of their rights
>   and withhold justice from the oppressed of my people,
> making widows their prey
>   and robbing the fatherless.

What will you do on the day of reckoning,
    when disaster comes from afar?
To whom will you run for help?
    Where will you leave your riches? (Is 10:1-3)

So yes, I will still pray for our political leaders that God will bring them
into meaningful confrontation with the gospel and to repentance and
salvation. I pray *for* them, but I also pray *against* them in relation to
policies and actions that are incompatible with biblical standards for
society. I think the Bible authorizes both kinds of prayer.

I see this paradox and combination in Daniel, again. He clearly de-
nounces the evil of the regime of Nebuchadnezzar, yet, as I suggested
before, he was almost certainly praying *for* Nebuchadnezzar (as Jer 29:7
instructs the exiles to do). Indeed, Daniel tries to help Nebuchadnezzar
avoid God's judgment by urging him to stop his oppression of the poor.
"Therefore, Your Majesty, be pleased to accept my advice: Renounce your
sins by doing what is right, and your wickedness by being kind to the
oppressed. It may be that then your prosperity will continue" (Dan 4:27).
In the midst of Daniel's prayer life, he received dramatic visions that made
him vividly aware of the satanic, idolatrous, bestially evil nature of the
political power of the governments that he lived under in Babylon and
Persia. Yet at the same time he was able to go on serving the human rulers
themselves in the midst of that culture. There is a remarkable spiritual
maturity and balance to be observed here. He knew the spiritual realities
of underlying idolatry and evil. Yet he could be fully engaged in the civic
and political workplace and public arena, while preserving the distinctiveness of his faith and ethic—a distinctiveness that brought on him
both grudging recognition and vicious hatred (Dan 6:1-5).

Daniel was a citizen of Zion, living in Babylon, a believer living in a
pagan political world. He knew that Babylon stood under God's wrath
for its outrageous arrogance, violence, and oppression. Yet he continued
to work, serve and pray, *right there in the midst of Babylon*—not with
naive admiration and sycophantic praise for its rulers but with godly
integrity, ethical distinctiveness, and daily prayer. Followers of Jesus

need to be people of prayer, with that kind of discernment and spiritual insight. We need to be fully conscious of the false gods and satanic evils that masquerade in the midst of the political realm, and yet able to go on working, serving, and witnessing with diligence and integrity, doing so as servants of God while serving those whom God permits to exercise authority in human society.

Conclusion

As the book of Revelation alerts us, Babylon is still the world we live in. It is a world of posttruth, fake news, contradictions and denials, then denials of denials; a world of utter confusion of sexual morals and the boasting approval of things even non-Christian society once deplored. It is a world where sexual predation is a perk of wealth and celebrity, where mockery and insult are the daily stock-in-trade of political discourse, where greed is good and not paying your taxes is smart. It is a world where the idolatry of the "strong man" has infected every continent, with diminishing accountability and increasingly condoned extrajudicial violence. It is a world of grossly obscene economic disparity, not just between the rich world and the so-called developing world but within most of our wealthy Western countries also. It is a world where the restraints of constitutional limits, accepted traditions of honor and integrity, and boundaries between political office and personal enrichment are ignored with apparent impunity. It is a world where the lobbying and propaganda power of vested interests have, for decades, so shaped political will and obstructed timely intervention that creation itself is groaning as both the victim and the instrument of God's judgment on human hubris. It is a world where still two-thirds of its population do not yet know and worship the one true living God of all the earth, and many millions have not even heard the name of his Son; a world still shamed by the spiritual injustice that some of us feel free to argue viciously over which of the innumerable English versions of the Bible conforms to our particular theological criteria, while millions of our sisters and brothers in Christ have no portion of God's Word at all as yet in their own language.

A fallen, broken, sinful, rebellious, turbulent, endangered, suffering world. A world in which the false gods and idols seem so sneeringly triumphant.

Yet it is in this same world that we are still called to be the followers of the *crucified* Lord. Ours is the mandate to lift up the cross of Christ and bear witness to him, to live and serve in the kingdom of God, which he inaugurated, and to proclaim the good news of all he taught, modeled, and gloriously accomplished in his death and resurrection. For it is in the cross of Christ that the uniqueness of the Christian faith most totally resides, and with it the utter singular uniqueness of the one true living God of the biblical revelation. It is ultimately in the light of the cross that all gods and idols are exposed for the despicable frauds they are.

We are to lift up that cross *precisely in this world of evil, folly, idolatry, and confusion*. For it was *in* such a world, and *for* such a world, that Jesus died and rose again, and calls us to follow him. In the words of George F. Macleod:

> I simply argue that the Cross be raised again at the centre of the market-place as well as on the steeple of the church. I am recovering the claim that Jesus was not crucified in a cathedral between two candles, but on a cross between two thieves; on the town garbage-heap; at a crossroad so cosmopolitan that they had to write his title in Hebrew and in Latin and in Greek . . . at the kind of place where cynics talk smut, and thieves curse, and soldiers gamble. Because that is where churchmen should be and what churchmanship should be about.[6]

EPILOGUE

THE DAYS IMMEDIATELY FOLLOWING the general election in the United Kingdom in December 2019 found me depressed and angry.[1] I had prayed fervently to the Lord on behalf of the poor, disabled, prisoners, homeless, children, and the elderly in social care, along with hospital staff, probation services, teachers, carers—all of whom have suffered worsening conditions of hardship in the accumulating impact of austerity policies and severe cuts across so many areas of our national life by the government that has been in office over the past decade. And it seemed God had neither answered my prayer nor heard their cry. My anger was directed not only at the blatant corruption and industrial-scale mendacity of our politics but also at our God, who seems, as Job put it in one of his most trenchantly challenging accusations, "charges no one with wrongdoing" (Job 24:12). And it seems there will be no respite in such policies for years to come, with the same government now with an increased parliamentary majority.[2] How does God tolerate it?

Along with those emotions at exactly the same time, my wife, Liz, and I were sharing the profound grief of so many at the tragic death in a horrific road accident in South Africa of Chris Naylor, international director of A Rocha, the Christian environmental and creation-care movement along with his wife Susanna.[3] The same accident also took the life of Miranda Harris, wife of Peter Harris, who was severely injured but survived. Peter and Miranda were the pioneering founders of A Rocha and dearly loved friends of ours for more than thirty years. "Why, Lord?" was the question on all our lips.

In this mixture of sorrow and anger, several days after the general election, I went with Liz to the Thanksgiving service for Miranda's life, held at Saint Aldate's Church, Oxford, where Miranda's brother-in-law Charlie Cleverley is the senior pastor and conducted the service. Hundreds of people filled the church from all over the country—and indeed from other countries. It was an overwhelming outpouring of thanks for her remarkable life and grief at the seemingly so untimely manner of it being snatched away from all who loved her.

Charlie Cleverley preached a powerful message from the psalms, in which—with reference of course to Miranda—he urged us to dwell on the importance of *lament*, the power of a life of *love*, and the reality of *hope*.

Lament, he urged, was not only understandable but biblically valid and even encouraged in the face of such inexplicable loss. With the psalmists, we cry out to God in protest and pain, and God does not turn a deaf ear. Charlie quoted an extract from a prayer that I myself had composed some days earlier in relation to the deaths of Miranda and the Naylors.

> Their death, Lord, is so grievous for us, for their families, for all who knew and loved them. This loss is so devastating, so sudden, so humanly tragic. So we lament, we mourn, we cry out in pain— we are baffled and bewildered.
>
> And we cry out to you in protest, Lord. Yes, even in protest as so many of the psalmists did as they struggled to understand your ways and your deeds. Why, O Lord, should such a terrible thing happen? Why did such an accident somehow find room within your sovereign and gracious providence and governance of all our lives? Why? Dear sovereign Lord, we do not expect or demand an answer, but we cannot spare you the question for it burns within us. We do not need an explanation, but we do need your reassurance and your presence and your comfort. Please help us, O Lord.

Love was personified in Miranda's life, as all who knew her could testify. And such a gift from God would bear fruit for eternity in ways that only

God could measure. Her life of love was for us to remember and celebrate and to emulate in whatever moments and opportunities God put
in our path.

And the sure and steadfast *hope* of sharing in the resurrection of
Christ and in the glorious life of the new creation sustains all of us who
believe in him, in the face of the death of loved ones or our own
eventual demise.

It was the perfect message for the occasion, delivered with a pastor's
heart, a brother's love, and the Bible's authority. But as I drank it in, I
found it speaking to my other grief—for our country; and to my other
anger—for those suffering the crushing impacts of impoverishment,
social neglect, and bureaucratic cruelties. Lament, love, and hope—
such profound biblical words for such a time as this, I thought.

For should I not *lament* that impoverishment in my country has increased to such an extent that, in this allegedly sixth-largest economy in
the world, there are now more food banks than McDonalds?[4] Should I
not protest at the stereotyping and stigmatizing of the poor that has ended,
for some, in starvation or suicide? Should I not lament that a third of
children in Britain are living in so much poverty (according the government's own official definition and metrics) that some schoolteachers
spend their own money to help the half-million children who come
hungry to school, and that 135,000 children were living with their families
in overcrowded temporary accommodations last Christmas, effectively
homeless because of cuts in housing benefits, soaring private rents, and
consequent evictions?[5] Surely the anger I feel at such realities in my own
country (as a grandparent trying to imagine what that would be like for
my own beloved grandchildren) must echo something of God's anger at
such injustice and inequality. Is it not a matter of national shame that cuts
to staff and funding in the prison service have led to gross deterioration
in conditions in many prisons, with overcrowding and filth, rampant drug
abuse, some prisoners locked up for twenty-three hours a day, and the
collapse of efforts at rehabilitation, reform, education, and training?[6]
Where is the God of justice, the God who sees, hears, and knows the

plight of widows, orphans, and prisoners—where is this God of the Bible when governments and the voting public turn a blind eye? Yes, I lament, and I join Psalms 10, 12, and 82, for example, in lodging my protest and complaint before the throne of the universe. How long, O Lord?

But then comes *love*. And this is where the energy of lament has to be transformed into action, and therein, of course, lies the challenge for myself as for any Christian with eyes to see and a heart to feel. For those who appeal to the righteousness of God must reflect his righteousness in their own lives, in kindness and generosity to the needy, as the psalmists also realized. Notice how, in the matching acrostic Psalms 111 and 112, the redeeming generosity of God is reflected in the compassion and generosity of those who fear him (e.g. Ps 111:3, 4, 5, 9; Ps 112:3, 4, 5, 9).

"The power of a life of love," was Charlie's phrase. What then could be the power of the lives of love of the combined multitudes of Christian believers in the country? Actually, Christian love is already powerfully at work and in evidence. Most of those food banks that outnumber McDonalds are run by churches, often in association with the Trussell Trust, a charity that provided 1.6 million emergency supplies in 2019 and is established on Christian principles and the words of Jesus in Matthew 25:35-36. "For I was hungry and you gave me something to eat, I was thirsty and you gave me something to drink, I was a stranger and you invited me in, I needed clothes and you clothed me, I was sick and you looked after me, I was in prison and you came to visit me."

But as I reflected on Charlie's phrase, it seems that the church as a whole will need to step-up even more, in living out "lives of love" that are the embodiment of the gospel itself. We have good news to share because there *is* good news of what God has done in the cross and resurrection of Christ to demonstrate God's own redeeming love and justice. The power of a life of love is in reality the power of the truth of the gospel. And we are gospel people or nothing at all.

Since the days of the Roman Empire, Christians were known for deeds of love and care for the needy, the sick, and the poor. In the centuries that followed, Christians have founded hospitals and schools and sought justice for the poor all over the world. Some of the first initiatives in mutual help and financial insurance against illness, poverty, and death were pioneered on Christian principles. And in contemporary Britain, Christians Against Poverty (CAP) is reputedly one of the most effective agencies helping many people out of the crushing tentacles of debt poverty.[7] So, yes, there is huge potential in the power of Christian lives of love, in a society where the state seems to have opted out of its biblical obligation to care for the poor and provide systemic redress for economic forces of impoverishment. I find this a personal challenge: to turn depression and anger into practical action of some kind, *any* kind, that responds to the evils of social and economic inequality and injustice with actions that palely reflect the example of Jesus. What can I do, what can you do, more than merely complaining about political authorities who *fail* to do what, according the Bible, they *should* do?

And finally *hope*? Ah, there's perhaps the hardest challenge of all. It is hard to be optimistic these days. The idols have come to rule, it seems— the idols of greed, arrogant narcissism, grand-scale relentless lying, ruthless authoritarian power manipulating a social-media pandemic of malicious misinformation and public gullibility, sycophantic politicians happy to sacrifice their consciences for personal or party advantage. It is hard to be optimistic when a single minibus could hold the number of men whose combined wealth is greater than the poorest half of the world's population or the twenty-two who own more wealth than all the women in Africa. It is hard to be optimistic when the breakdown of earth's climate systems threatens to make some parts of the planet uninhabitable through excessive heat, inundation by rising sea levels, or recurring drought.

Hard to be optimistic, yes. But then, biblical Christian hope was never mere optimism. Optimism imagines that things will get better— eventually. Christian hope knows that things may well get much worse (indeed Jesus said that they would), *but* God is still sovereign, and God is good, and God is just. Christian hope knows that the future belongs to the kingdom of God. Christian hope knows that the judge of all the earth will do right. Evil will not have the last word. God will ultimately judge the wicked and vindicate the righteous. For that reason, the Day of Judgment is part of the gospel (Rom 2:16)—the ultimate rectification, when all wrongs will be dealt with. God will put all things right before God makes all things new. That is good news!

So yes, there is hope—solid sustaining biblical hope. It is not surprising that Paul connects hope so closely with both faith and love. For we need the faith to believe it and the love to embody it.

And that is why corporate worship is so important. It is faithful, regular participation with God's people in the rhythm of praise and prayer that expresses and reinforces faith, inspires and channels love, and sustains hope. And once again the psalms become our companion.

For me, that afternoon at Saint Aldate's Church in Oxford was a Psalm 73 moment. The psalmist, like me, was wallowing in agonized grumbling and fuming about the success of the wicked, their arrogant boasting, and apparent impunity. What is the point of being honest and godly when the world favors the liars and cheats? Such were his bitter thoughts until, he tells us, "I entered the sanctuary of God" (Ps 73:17). And there, in the context of worship, he experiences a reorientation of his perspective. He sees that the wicked are indeed in a very dangerous place—under the impending judgment of God. And he sees that there is ultimate security in knowing and trusting the living God and finding refuge in him. That is where his hope lies—both for the present and even "afterward you will take me into glory" (Ps 73:24).

But the psalms hold out more than personal hope. They also affirm very robustly that God will ultimately do justice on earth. Even the intensely personal rescue of Psalm 34 affirms the wider truth that "the LORD is close to the brokenhearted and saves those who are crushed in spirit" (Ps 34:18).

It was undoubtedly an eschatological conviction that lay beyond the lifetime of David and still lies beyond our own, that "evil will slay the wicked; the foes of the righteous will be condemned. The LORD will rescue his servants; no one who takes refuge in him will be condemned" (Ps 34:21-22).

And as I said, the future belongs to the kingdom of God, and when the psalms of God's kingship get into full flow, they envisage the whole of creation celebrating with joy when the Lord, the earth's true king and judge, comes to judge the earth, which means to put all things right.

> Say among the nations, "The LORD reigns."
>> The world is firmly established, it cannot be moved;
>> he will judge the peoples with equity.
>
> Let the heavens rejoice, let the earth be glad;
>> let the sea resound, and all that is in it.
> Let the fields be jubilant, and everything in them;
>> let all the trees of the forest sing for joy.
> Let all creation rejoice before the LORD, for he comes,
>> he comes to judge the earth.
> He will judge the world in righteousness
>> and the peoples in his faithfulness. (Ps 96:10-13)

That is the hope that regular worship sustains, the only hope that staves off despair in the face of increasing social wickedness and political folly, the accumulating slag heap of crushed and brokenhearted suffering, and the groaning of creation itself. For, to be honest, I still struggle with the temptation to give in to cynicism and despair. If it is hard to be optimistic, it is all too easy to be paralyzingly pessimistic. And that is not a Christian option either.

Charlie Cleverley was right to respond to Miranda Harris's tragic death with words of lament, love, and hope, and to do so with tears of trust in the sovereignty and goodness of our heavenly Father. And on a wider canvas we, too, are called to lament, and to love, and to hope. We do so not just for two bereaved families but on behalf of our neighborhoods, our countries, and our world with the tenacity of trust in the compassion and ultimate justice of creation's Lord and King.

May your kingdom come. May your will be done on earth as in heaven.

Maranatha. Come, Lord Jesus.

NOTES

Part one: the Lord God and other gods in the Bible

[1]These opening paragraphs are a very summarizing reference back to the previous two chapters of my *The Mission of God: Unlocking the Bible's Grand Narrative* (Downers Grove, IL: InterVarsity Press, 2006), "The Living God Makes Himself Known in Israel" and "The Living God Makes Himself Known in Jesus Christ."

1 The paradox of the gods

[1]Robert Karl Gnuse, *No Other Gods: Emergent Monotheism in Israel*, Journal for the Study of the Old Testament Supplement Series 241 (Sheffield: Sheffield Academic Press, 1997). Gnuse's study, of course, is only one of a very large number of scholarly explorations of the origins and history of monotheism in Israelite religion, and its bibliography is a useful guide to that literature.

[2]Yair Hoffman, "The Concept of 'Other Gods' in the Deuteronomistic Literature," in *Politics and Theopolitics*, ed. Henning Graf Reventlow, Yair Hoffman, and Benjamin Uffenheimer (Sheffield: Sheffield Academic, 1994), 66-84, 70-71.

[3]For a general critique of this evolutionary view of Israel's religion, and the historical reconstruction on which it is based, see Richard Bauckham, "Biblical Theology and the Problems of Monotheism," in *Out of Egypt: Biblical Theology and Biblical Interpretation*, ed. Craig Bartholomew, Mary Healy, Karl Möller, Robin Parry, and Anthony C. Thiselton (Grand Rapids: Zondervan, 2004), 187-232.

[4]Bauckham, "Biblical Theology," 196.

[5]Bauckham, "Biblical Theology," 211.

[6]In my view it is significant that Deut 4:19 does not explicitly say that God apportioned the heavenly bodies *to be worshiped* (those words are not in the Hebrew). He simply gave these gifts of creation to all nations—which included Israel. That other nations do in fact worship them is not to be imitated by Israel.

[7]From the hymn "Facing a Task Unfinished," by Frank Houghton, © OMF; quoted with permission.

2 What are the gods?

[1]Gordon D. Fee, *The First Epistle to the Corinthians*, New International Commentary on the New Testament (Grand Rapids: Eerdmans, 1987), 472.

[2]Hebrew *šēdîm*. This rare word is found only here and in Ps 106:37. It is cognate with the Akkadian word *sedu*, which in ancient Mesopotamian religion referred to protective spirits associated with the dead. The association with human sacrifice, mentioned in Ps 106, is also attested in Mesopotamian religion.

[3]Psalm 96:5, for example, speaks of the worship of the non-Israelite peoples and dismisses their gods as *'ĕlîlîm*. On this occasion, the Septuagint translated that term with *daimonia*—"demons." But elsewhere the word *'ĕlîlîm* does not necessarily mean demons but refers rather to something worthless, weak, powerless, useless, of no value.

[4]Brian Wintle, "A Biblical Perspective on Idolatry," in *The Indian Church in Context: Her Emergence, Growth and Mission*, ed. Mark T. B. Laing (Delhi: CMS/ISPCK, 2003), 60.

[5]The Deuteronomic historian's point here in the mouth of Hezekiah echoes the same assessment of idols that is made in Deut 4:28.

[6]John Barton, "'The Work of Human Hands' (Ps 115:4): Idolatry in the Old Testament," *Ex Auditu* 15 (1999): 67.

[7]See, for example, the pluralist perspective in W. Cantwell Smith, "Idolatry in Comparative Perspective," in *The Myth of Christian Uniqueness*, ed. J. Hick and P. F. Knitter (Maryknoll, NY: Orbis Books, 1987), 53-68.

[8]Barton, "'Work of Human Hands,'" 66, italics added.

[9]I would not view the difference between Hosea and Isaiah in the terms Barton expresses it. I doubt whether Hosea imagined that the other gods of the nations with whom Israel was getting politically entangled had objective divine-reality alternative to Yahweh any more than Isaiah did (particularly in view of the way he also dismisses them as human products in Hos 8:4, 6; 13:2; 14:3). So while I believe Barton rightly understands Isaiah's meaning, I am not convinced it was such a breakthrough as he makes out.

[10]This state of affairs is exposed in the revealing indignation of the priest of Bethel against what he regarded as the seditious prophecies of Amos: "this is *the king's* sanctuary and the temple of *the kingdom*" (Amos 7:13).

[11]See for example the survey provided by Morton Smith, "The Common Theology of the Ancient Near East," in *Essential Papers on Israel and the Ancient Near East*, ed. F. E. Greenspan (New York: New York University Press, 1991), 49-65. Smith, however, goes on to minimize any specific distinctiveness in the faith of Israel.

[12]From Joachim Neander's hymn "All My Hope on God Is Founded" (written in 1680 and translated by Robert Bridges in 1899).

3 Discerning the gods

[1]Jacques Ellul was one of the earliest to connect biblical categories of idolatry with contemporary Western cultural trends, especially secularism. He analyzes the sacred and symbolic aspects of technique, sex, the nation-state, revolution, and the mythology of history and science. See Ellul, *The New Demons* (London: Mowbrays, 1976). J. A. Walter applied the same methodology to a range of social phenomena, many of which appear good in themselves but easily become elevated to idolatrous status, such as work, the family, suburbia, individualism, ecology, race, and the media. See Walter, *A Long Way from Home: A Sociological Exploration of Contemporary Idolatry* (Carlisle, UK: Paternoster, 1979). Bob Goudzwaard extended the analysis to the whole realm of ideology, focusing especially on the ideologies of revolution, the nation, material prosperity, and guaranteed security. See Goudzwaard, *Idols of Our Time* (Downers Grove, IL: InterVarsity Press, 1984). Walter Wink's trilogy is one of the most extensive studies of the "powers" in biblical (and especially New Testament) thought but is criticized for not giving sufficient weight to the biblical assertions about the objective demonic aspects of their infiltration of human structures. See Wink, *Naming the Powers: The Language of Power in the New Testament* (Philadelphia: Fortress, 1984); Wink, *Unmasking the Powers: The Invisible Forces That Determine Human Existence* (Philadelphia: Fortress, 1986); Wink, *Engaging the Powers: Discernment and Resistance in a World of Domination* (Minneapolis: Fortress, 1992). Clinton Arnold is more balanced in that respect. See Arnold, *Powers of Darkness: A Thoughtful, Biblical Look at an Urgent Challenge Facing the Church* (Downers Grove, IL: InterVarsity Press, 1992). Vinoth Ramachandra presses the analysis of modernity and its sequel further in observing the violence of the new idolatries, the dogmatism of those who idolize science, and the continuing idolatry of "reason and unreason." See Ramachandra, *Gods That Fail: Modern Idolatry and Christian Mission* (Carlisle, UK: Paternoster, 1996). Peter Moore tackles the various idolatries of Western culture in a more apologetic mode, addressing those who may be dazzled by them—including New Age-ism, relativism, narcissism, and hedonism. See Moore, *Disarming the Secular Gods* (Downers Grove, IL: InterVarsity Press, 1989). Craig Bartholomew and Thorsten Moritz edit a volume in which a number of biblical scholars examine consumerism as a form of contemporary idolatry. See Bartholomew and Moritz, eds., *Christ and Consumerism: A Critical Analysis of the Spirit of the Age* (Carlisle, UK: Paternoster, 2000). Bruce Ashford and Heath Thomas explore the implications of biblical monotheism as it confronts the idolatries of secularism, individualism, and cultural decadence. See Ashford

and Thomas, *The Gospel of Our King: Bible, Worldview, and the Mission of Every Christian* (Grand Rapids: Baker Academic, 2019).

[2] The language of idolatry is commonly and cheerfully used in the context of TV and movies in Western culture when the media pours adulation on celebrities as pop and fashion idols and sex goddesses.

[3] For example, Marvin E. Tate says: "I have read v 6 as expressing the great qualities of Yahweh's kingship as personifications, who attend him in the temple (cf. Ps 85:14; 89:15). The entourage of Yahweh is not made up of a company of lesser gods, who are in reality no gods, but those 'agents' of his own which are manifest in his saving work and wondrous deeds." Tate, *Psalms 51–100*, Word Biblical Commentary 20 (Dallas: Word Books, 1990), 514.

[4] From the hymn by Nahum Tate (1682–1715), "Through All the Changing Scenes of Life."

[5] Since the original writing of this sentence, of course, the world has been devastated by the coronavirus Covid-19, which has needed no media hype to spread its fear. So I am not at all suggesting that such a pandemic is not a terrible reality and rightly to be feared; but rather, that its impact exposes some of the follies and idols in human behavior globally that may have led to the viral transfer from animals to humans, and some of the political arrogance and complacency that exacerbated its lethal grip in some countries.

[6] Jeremiah scornfully reverses the gender of the idolatry here: the wooden pole was the female, maternal symbol, while the standing stone was the male, phallic symbol.

[7] From the editorial "It Must Be Someone's Fault—It Might Be Our Own," *Independent on Sunday*, February 28, 1993, in the wake of the murder of two-year-old James Bulger by two ten-year-old children.

4 Mission and the gods

[1] Johannes Verkuyl, *Contemporary Missiology: An Introduction* (Grand Rapids: Eerdmans, 1978), 95. See also, as a serious treatment of conflict as an essential element of mission in biblical thought, Marc R. Spindler, *La Mission: Combat Pour Le Salut Du Monde* (Neuchatel: Delachaux & Niestle, 1967).

[2] Robert B. Chisholm also observes these three broadly significant eras in the conflict between Yahweh and the gods, and then concentrates on the latter two. See Chisholm, "'To Whom Shall You Compare Me?' Yahweh's Polemic Against Baal and the Babylonian Idol-Gods in Prophetic Literature," in *Christianity and the Religions: A Biblical Theology of World Religions*, ed. E. Rommen and H. A. Netland (Pasadena, CA: William Carey Library, 1995), 56-71.

[3] For this reading of the situation in Acts 17, see Bruce Winter, "On Introducing Gods to Athens: An Alternative Reading of Acts 17:18-20," *Tyndale Bulletin* 47 (1996):

71-90. The phrase "introducing new gods into Athens" is formalized like this because it was a potentially criminal offense if the one introducing new gods could not justify it. It was part of the charge that led to the execution of Socrates. Paul was in a vulnerable situation.

[4]This is an unusual but richly meaningful metaphor for the covenant relationship. In its intimacy and mutuality, it is like the bond between a person and a favorite piece of clothing that is bound affectionately and tightly to one's body. The covenant is God wearing his people.

Part two: political idolatry then and now

[1]With the famous retort "We don't do God" at a press conference in May 2003, Alistair Campbell, senior adviser to then–British Prime Minister Tony Blair, prevented Blair from answering a question about the religious faith he shared with President George W. Bush and whether they prayed together.

5 The rise and fall of nations in biblical perspective

[1]For a more in-depth discussion of the sovereignty of God in the world of nations and how that connects with God's purpose for all nations through Old Testament Israel, see my *The Mission of God: Unlocking the Bible's Grand Narrative* (Downers Grove, IL: InterVarsity Press, 2006), chap. 14, "God and the Nations in Old Testament Vision."

[2]Adelaide A. Potter, "Have Thine Own Way, Lord" (1907).

[3]Nobody knows for sure how many Christians there are today in mainland China, but estimates vary between 80 and more than 100 million.

[4]See Minderoo Foundation, Global Slavery Index, www.globalslaveryindex.org (accessed December 4, 2019).

[5]On clothing, see Josephine Moulds, "Child Labour in the Fashion Supply Chain," *Guardian*, https://labs.theguardian.com/unicef-child-labour/ (accessed December 4, 2019). On cell phones, see Annie Kelly, "Children as Young as Seven Mining Cobalt Used in Smartphones, Says Amnesty," *Guardian*, January 18, 2016, www.theguardian .com/global-development/2016/jan/19/children-as-young-as-seven-mining-cobalt -for-use-in-smartphones-says-amnesty/. On food, see Annie Kelly, "Thai Seafood: Are the Prawns on Your Plate Still Fished by Slaves?," *Guardian*, January 23, 2018, www .theguardian.com/global-development/2018/jan/23/thai-seafood-industry-report -trafficking-rights-abuses/.

[6]Many of the most intractable and tragic conflicts in today's world have their roots in oppressive, racist, and self-serving political decisions, policies, and interventions by colonial powers in previous centuries: this can be traced in the Middle East, Northern

Ireland, Rwanda, the Rohingya in Myanmar, the Indian subcontinent, Sri Lanka, and doubtless many more.

[7]See Child Poverty Action Group, "Child Poverty Facts and Figures," March 2019, https://cpag.org.uk/child-poverty/child-poverty-facts-and-figures/.

[8]See Poverty USA, "The Population of Poverty USA," www.povertyusa.org/facts/ (accessed December 4, 2019).

[9]See Larry Elliott, "World's 26 Richest People Own as Much as Poorest 50%, Says Oxfam," *Guardian*, January 20, 2019, www.theguardian.com/business/2019/jan/21 /world-26-richest-people-own-as-much-as-poorest-50-per-cent-oxfam-report/.

[10]See, e.g., Silje Pileberg, "Inequality May Lead to Violence and Extremism," UiO Department of Psychology, July 7, 2017, www.sv.uio.no/psi/english/research/news-and -events/news/inequality-may-lead-to-violence-and-extremism.html; "'It Has Been Proven, Less Inequality Means Less Crime,'" World Bank, September 5, 2014, www .worldbank.org/en/news/feature/2014/09/03/latinoamerica-menos-desigualdad -se-reduce-el-crimen/.

[11]See "Effects of Economic Inequality," Wikipedia, https://en.wikipedia.org/wiki /Effects_of_economic_inequality/(accessed December 4, 2019).

[12]In saying that I believe same-sex intercourse should not be treated as a *crime* by the state (and that I therefore welcome its decriminalization in the West and regret its continued criminal status in other parts of the world), I am not questioning what I regard as the Bible's *ethical* teaching on human sexuality, within which same-sex genital intimacy is throughout portrayed as not pleasing to God.

[13]See, e.g., Alysse ElHage, "When It Comes to Child Well-Being, Is One Parent the Same as Two?," Institute for Family Studies, September 7, 2017, https://ifstudies.org/blog /when-it-comes-to-child-well-being-is-one-parent-the-same-as-two/; Branwen Jeffreys, "Do Children in Two-Parent Families Do Better?," BBC News, February 5, 2019, www.bbc.co.uk/news/education-47057787/.

[14]See "Cost of Family Breakdown," Marriage Foundation, https://marriagefoundation .org.uk/research/cost-of-family-breakdown/ (accessed December 5, 2019).

[15]See "Climate Change and Poverty," Wikipedia, https://en.wikipedia.org/wiki /Climate_change_and_poverty/(accessed December 5, 2019); Robert Mendelsohn, Ariel Dinar, and Larry Williams, "The Distributional Impact of Climate Change on Rich and Poor Countries," *Environment and Development Economics* 11, no. 2 (April 2006), https://doi.org/10.1017/S1355770X05002755.

[16]See, e.g., "ExxonMobil Climate Change Controversy," Wikipedia, https://en.wikipedia .org/wiki/ExxonMobil_climate_change_controversy/(accessed December 5, 2019); Susanne Rust, "Report Details How ExxonMobil and Fossil Fuel Firms Sowed Seeds of Doubt on Climate Change," *Los Angeles Times*, October 21, 2019, www.latimes.com

/environment/story/2019-10-21/oil-companies-exxon-climate-change-denial
-report/; accessed December 5, 2019; Jane Meyer, "'Kochland' Examines the Koch
Brothers' Early, Crucial Role in Climate-Change Denial," *New Yorker*, August 13, 2019,
www.newyorker.com/news/daily-comment/kochland-examines-how-the-koch
-brothers-made-their-fortune-and-the-influence-it-bought/.

[17]See, e.g., Jim Waterson, "Uncovered: Reality of How Smartphones Turned Election
News into Chaos," *Guardian*, December 5, 2019, www.theguardian.com/politics/2019
/dec/05/uncovered-reality-of-how-smartphones-turned-election-news-into-chaos/.

[18]The saying seems to have been a widely used proverb that Spurgeon quoted in a
sermon in 1855. See "'Joseph Attacked by the Archers': A Sermon Delivered April 1,
1855," in *Sermons Delivered in Exeter Hall, Strand by Rev. C. H. Spurgeon (Charles
Haddon Spurgeon)* (London: Alabaster & Passmore, 1855).

[19]My own doctoral research was in this area, and for more detail on what the Old Testament has to say on issues of political, social, economic, and other areas of life, and
the principles by which we may legitimately apply such material in today's societies,
see my book *Old Testament Ethics for the People of God* (Downers Grove, IL: Inter-
Varsity Press, 2004).

6 God in the political arena

[1]Christopher J. H. Wright, *Old Testament Ethics for the People of God* (Downers Grove,
IL: InterVarsity Press, 2004), 212-26.

[2]See, e.g., Camilo Maldonado, "Trump Tax Cuts Helped Billionaires Pay Less Taxes
than the Working Class in 2018," Forbes, October 10, 2019, www.forbes.com/sites
/camilomaldonado/2019/10/10/trump-tax-cuts-helped-billionaires-pay-less-taxes-
than-the-working-class-in-2018/#713a310e3128; Taylor Nicole Rogers, "American
Billionaires Paid Less in Taxes in 2018 than the Working Class, Analysis Shows—and
It's Another Sign That One of the Biggest Problems in the US Is Only Getting Worse,"
Business Insider, October 9, 2019, www.businessinsider.com/american-billionaires
-paid-less-taxes-than-working-class-wealth-gap-2019-10?r=US&IR=T.

[3]In relation to the United Kingdom, see "Lobbying," Transparency International UK,
www.transparency.org.uk/our-work/uk-corruption/lobbying/ (accessed December
5, 2019); Adam Ramsay, "Welcome to Boris Johnson's Government of All the Lobbyists," Open Democracy, July 27, 2019, www.opendemocracy.net/en/opendemocracy
uk/welcome-to-boris-johnsons-government-of-all-the-lobbyists/. On the power of
corporations in the United States, see Senator Sheldon Whitehouse with Melanie
Wachtell Stinnett, *Captured: The Corporate Infiltration of American Democracy* (New
York: The New Press, 2019); and, e.g., John Perry, "Corporations and the Future of
Democracy," *Philosophy Talk* (blog), October 9, 2014, www.philosophytalk.org/blog

/corporations-and-future-democracy; Liz Kennedy, "Corporate Capture Threatens Democratic Government," American Progress, March, 29, 2017, www.american progress.org/issues/democracy/news/2017/03/29/429442/corporate-capture -threatens-democratic-government/.

[4]See Christopher J. H. Wright, *Hearing the Message of Daniel* (Grand Rapids: Zondervan, 2017), 114.

[5]The United States, for example, spends more on defense than the next seven countries combined: China, Saudi Arabia, India, France, Russia, the United Kingdom, and Germany. See "U.S. Defense Spending Compared to Other Countries," Peter G. Peterson Foundation, May 3, 2019, www.pgpf.org/chart-archive/0053_defense-comparison/.

[6]Mass shootings in the United States in 2019 outnumbered the number of days in the year. Now happening more than once a day and defined as "an incident where four or more people are shot in a single shooting spree," they claimed 441 lives out of a total of 1,907 victims. See "List of Mass Shootings in the United States in 2019," Wikipedia, https://en.wikipedia.org/wiki/List_of_mass_shootings_in_the_United_States_in _2019/(accessed December 5, 2019).

[7]Just go to Amazon and search "gods guns and guts," www.amazon.com/s?k=god +guns+and+guts&ref=nb_sb_noss_1 (accessed December 5, 2019). Or Google "Images for god guns and guts" to find the vast range of merchandise on offer.

[8]For a survey of some helpful books that explore the idols of contemporary Western culture and politics, see the footnote at the beginning of chapter 3 above.

[9]The hermeneutical assumptions and a wide variety of contexts of ethical application are explored in much greater depth in Wright, *Old Testament Ethics for the People of God*.

[10]This is a popular paraphrase of Calvin rather than a precise quote. What he did say goes, "They who rule unjustly and incompetently have been raised up by him to punish the wickedness of the people" (*Institutes of the Christian Religion* 4.20.25). See Bill Muehlenberg, "Calvin on Wicked Rulers and God's Judgment," *CultureWatch* (blog), February 27, 2016, https://billmuehlenberg.com/2016/02/27/calvin-on-wicked-rulers -and-gods-judgment/.

7 A people shaped by the living God

[1]This is an expansion to seven acts of the very helpful outline of the Bible story as a drama in six acts, presented by Craig G. Bartholomew and Michael W. Goheen, *The Drama of Scripture: Finding Our Place in the Biblical Story*, 2nd ed. (Grand Rapids: Baker, 2014). I have inserted final judgment as a distinct act of rectification between the mission of the church in act 5 and the new creation in act 7. The idea of the symbols to represent each act is modified from an original set of "True Story Symbols," by Chris Gonzalez, Pastor of Missio Dei Community Church, Tempe, Arizona.

[2]On the day of writing this, Mark Carney, formerly governor of the Bank of England and now the United Nations special envoy on climate change and finance, said this in a radio interview: "We must bring the future into the present as a catalyst for action today." That is precisely what the Bible story does. It holds before our eyes the ultimate future—both as warning and as encouragement—in order to generate action in the present.

[3]The term goes back to the Anglican Consultative Council, 1984, and was adopted by the Lambeth Conference of Bishops in 1988. See Anglican Consultative Council, "Bonds of Affection—1984," 49; and "History of the Five Marks of Mission," Anglican Communion, www.anglicancommunion.org/mission/marks-of-mission.aspx (accessed December 31, 2019).

[4]Lausanne Movement, The Cape Town Commitment, I.7a, 2010, www.lausanne.org /content/ctc/ctcommitment/. This is the statement from the Third Lausanne Congress on World Evangelization, Cape Town, 2010.

[5]I have tried to give as full and comprehensive account as I can of what I believe to be a biblical understanding of mission, and what it means for the church to be the people of God for the sake of the mission of God, in various writings, including *The Mission of God: Unlocking the Bible's Grand Narrative* (Downers Grove, IL: InterVarsity Press, 2006); *The Mission of God's People: A Biblical Theology of the Church's Mission* (Grand Rapids: Zondervan, 2010); "Participatory Mission: The Mission of God's People Revealed in the Whole Bible Story," in *Four Views on the Church's Mission*, ed. Jason S. Sexton (Grand Rapids: Zondervan, 2017), 63-91; *Five Marks of Mission: Making God's Mission Ours* (Winchester, UK: im:press, 2015).

[6]Christopher J. H. Wright, "Jesus and His Old Testament Values," in *Knowing God Through the Old Testament: Three Volumes in One* (Downers Grove, IL: IVP Academic, 2019), 156-213.

[7]Wright, "Jesus and His Old Testament Values," 211-12.

[8]I have surveyed in depth the extent to which the ethical teaching of Jesus was rooted in the Old Testament Scriptures (in the Torah, the Prophets, Psalms, and wisdom), including the meaning and demands of the reign of God, in "Jesus and His Old Testament Values."

[9]In this all too hasty and negative sketch, I do not want to overlook that there were countermovements from below throughout the centuries of Christendom that sought to preserve a more Christlike witness to the truth of the gospel and the values of the kingdom of God—and often paid a high price for doing so. Nor am I unaware that, in the providence and sovereignty of God, there are positive dimensions to the legacy of Christendom. Paradoxically, as Tom Holland has pointed out in such historical depth and detail, it was this Christian saturation of European culture that inculcated many of the core values within the very system of beliefs now embraced and trumpeted as

Western liberalism, by which secularists critique and condemn Christianity in theory and practice. See Holland, *Dominion: The Making of the Western Mind* (London: Little, Brown, 2019).

[10]Again, I stress, this is not to say that we should not be glad if a Christian is elected president or prime minister. The danger is when we load *any* head of state who happens to be a Christian with a quasi-messianic expectation that they will right all wrongs, or that they will implement all our Christian ideals for society, or that they will remain totally uncontaminated by the corruption of our political systems, not to mention their own personal sinfulness, or that they will necessarily have superior political wisdom to a non-Christian in the same position. The history of Christians (including evangelicals) in high office, with a few exceptions (rather like the history of the kings of Israel), severely tempers such expectations.

[11]They are known as the Windrush generation, after the ship *Empire Windrush*, which brought some of the first West Indian immigrants to the United Kingdom in 1948. See "Windrush Scandal," Wikipedia, https://en.wikipedia.org/wiki/Windrush_scandal/ (accessed January 2, 2020).

[12]The Old Testament has a comprehensive economic message, including subtle analysis of the causes of poverty and systemic socioeconomic measures to address and redress it. Indeed, there is a depth and density of its attention to economic issues that is comparable to its supreme concern with the primal evil of idolatry—undoubtedly because there is such overlap between the two realms. I have surveyed, with extensive additional bibliography, the scope of Old Testament economic ethics including Israel's response to poverty in "Economics and the Poor," in *Old Testament Ethics for the People of God* (Downers Grove, IL: IVP Academic, 2004), 146-81.

8 Following Jesus in turbulent times

[1]The word translated "good" is *kalos*, which also means "beautiful," not just morally upright.

[2]I have explored more fully the biblical basis and missional implications of this combined call to engagement and distinctiveness in "People Who Live and Work in the Public Square," in *The Mission of God's People: A Biblical Theology of the Church's Mission* (Grand Rapids: Zondervan, 2010), 222-43. Other commendable books on the robust biblical theology of work and the importance to God of the workplace within his creational and redemptive purposes include Michael Wittmer, *Heaven Is a Place on Earth: Why Everything You Do Matters to God* (Grand Rapids: Zondervan, 2004); Darrell Cosden, *The Heavenly Good of Earthly Work* (Peabody, MA: Hendrickson, 2006); Tim Keller, *Every Good Endeavour: Connecting Your Work to God's Plan for the World* (London: Penguin Books, 2014).

[3]This is my own paraphrasing summary of a point I heard John Stott make on many occasions. For a fuller exposition of Stott's understanding of Christian social engagement and distinctiveness, see John Stott, *Christian Counter-Culture: The Message of the Sermon on the Mount* (Downers Grove, IL: InterVarsity Press, 1978), 57-68; Stott, "Our Plural World: Is Christian Witness Influential?," in *Issues Facing Christians Today*, 4th ed., rev. and updated by Roy McCloughry (Grand Rapids: Zondervan, 1978), 71-94.

[4]Lausanne Movement, The Cape Town Commitment, IIE.1, 2010, www.lausanne.org /content/ctc/ctcommitment/.

[5]The whole prayer can very properly be explored for its social and political significance— even though it is so often used only in contexts of private or liturgical worship. For reasons of space we can only here reflect on the implications of a few of its opening lines.

[6]George F. MacLeod, founder of the Iona Community. This now-famous quote is from his Cunningham Lectures, delivered in 1954 in New College, Edinburgh, and quoted in Ron Ferguson's *George MacLeod: Founder of the Iona Community* (Glasgow, UK: Wild Goose Publications, 2001), 265. The term *churchmen* and *churchmanship*, before the need for gender-inclusive terminology, were in common use at the time for active confessing Christians and committed membership of a local church.

Epilogue

[1]It is obvious that this epilogue reflects my personal location in the United Kingdom. I hope, however, that the issues and concerns it highlights are recognizable as relevant in many other contexts. It should also be stressed that this is a sincerely personal perspective. I have good Christian friends who take a different political position to my own, whom I love and respect. But I try to educate my political emotions with as much biblical and theological reflection as I can muster.

[2]The word *parliamentary* is important. The curiously unjust effect of our first-past-the-post system of elections in the UK means that, though the conservative party won a minority of actual votes cast (43%), they gained an eighty-seat majority in Parliament.

[3]A Rocha International, http://www.arocha.org.

[4]This is a fact. There are around 1,300 McDonald's outlets in the UK. There are now more than two thousand food banks. The number has risen astronomically since 2010.

[5]Another fact. "A Child in Britain Becomes Homeless Every Eight Minutes New Shelter Report Finds," *Newsround*, December 3, 2019, www.bbc.co.uk/newsround/50631620/.

[6]See, "Prisons," Institute for Government, accessed on February 10, 2020, www.institute forgovernment.org.uk/publication/performance-tracker-2019/prisons/.

[7]CAP has won awards for its effectiveness. See https://en.wikipedia.org/wiki/Christians _Against_Poverty/ and https://www.cashfloat.co.uk/blog/money-borrowing/christians -against-poverty-solution/.

SCRIPTURE INDEX

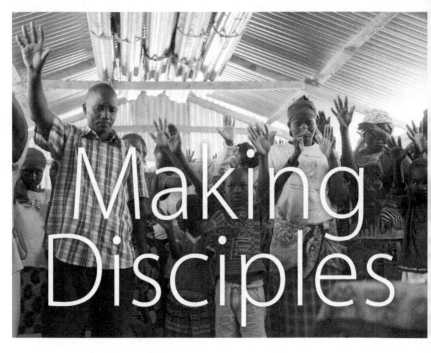

Around the World — Christianity is exploding
with growth in numbers

Yet — Believers are struggling to grow in Christ

That's Why Langham Exists

Our Vision

To see churches in the Majority World equipped for mission
and growing to maturity in Christ through the ministry of pastors
and leaders who believe, teach and live by the Word of God.

www.langham.org

FOUNDED BY JOHN STOTT

Langham PARTNERSHIP